Praise for
*Making Your Second Marriage
a First-Class Success*

"Anyone who is serious about having a strong and vibrant relationship will find practical and useful support in this book. I recommend it heartily."

—Ann Mortifee, dramatist, singer, Order of Canada

"The Moseleys beautifully articulate the dilemmas of both men and women. Their riveting stories helped me see myself; their insights are deep, fair-minded, and highly useful; and their approach is realistic, comprehensive, and hopeful. I also enjoyed their flashes of humor."

**—Jane Myers Drew, Ph.D.,
author of *Where Were You When I Needed You, Dad?***

"This is a much needed book that will surely help build a better foundation the second time around."

**—Gerald G. Jampolsky, M.D.,
author of *Love Is Letting Go of Fear***

"The Moseleys have written a book that will truly make a positive difference for those couples who are willing to listen to their wisdom. Their book is provocative and interesting reading and offers valuable illustrations of both the challenges and rewards of developing deeper connections with ourselves and our mates."

—Todd Creager, L.C.S.W., M.F.C.C.

"This wise and practical guide to the issues that must be addressed if your marriage is to be fulfilling is easy-to-read yet profound in its implications. If you are in a second marriage or considering embarking upon one and wish to benefit from the insights of those who have succeeded before you and to avoid repeating mistakes from your own past, buy this book, read it, and apply it."

—David Feinstein, Ph.D., author of *The Mythic Path*

"My marriage is the toughest thing I've ever had to do. The Moseleys know how true that is and address it with tremendous insight, warmth, and integrity. I feel delighted, greatly relieved, and filled with hope after reading their new book. And I cannot thank them enough for their guidance."

—Stephen Foster, film and television producer

"It becomes very clear when you read this book that Doug and Naomi Moseley know a lot about relationships. I was very impressed with the depth of knowledge, the down-to-earth practicality, and the astute approach taken in this book."

—Pat Love, Ed.D.

Making Your Second Marriage a First-Class Success

Doug and Naomi Moseley

 THREE RIVERS PRESS • NEW YORK

Published by Three Rivers Press, New York, New York.
Member of the Crown Publishing Group, a division of Random House, Inc., New York.
www.crownpublishing.com

THREE RIVERS PRESS and the Tugboat design are registered trademarks of Random House, Inc.

Originally published by Prima Publishing, Roseville, California, in 1998.

Printed in the United States of America

Library of Congress Cataloging-in-Publication Data

Moseley, Douglas.
    Making your second marriage a first-class success / Doug Moseley and Naomi Moseley.
        p.   cm.
    Includes bibliographical references and index.
    1. Remarriage. I. Moseley, Naomi. II. Title.
    HQ1018.M67   1998
    306.84—dc21   98-22822
                                                                        CIP

ISBN 0-7615-1424-4

10 9 8 7
First Edition

Danny and Josh Dworkis,
for all they have taught us

Contents

Acknowledgments

Special thanks go to Paula Munier Lee and Ethan Ellenburg, our agent, for their work in conceiving the project. We appreciate Susan Silva for nursing the book along and Leslie Eschen for her wonderful editing skills.

The support of Stephen Foster and Jane Mortifee was immeasurable. John Niendorff played a key role in shaping the material. Thanks also go to Mik and Laura Madsen, John Blaxall and Deepa Narayan, Mary Ann and Greg Hillman, and Krysta Kavenaugh and Gerry Brown for their input at key points. Most of all we are grateful to all our clients and friends who have many, many times offered us their vulnerability and truth and whose input made this book possible.

Introduction

If you are now in (or are considering entering) a second* marriage, this book is for you. If you have known the pain of a broken marriage and have the desire to make things different next time, this book is for you. If you are experienced in relationships and want to explore intimacy dynamics in a deeper way than you have before, this book is for you.

A Word about Our Approach

We are relationship counselors who are married to each other and have both been married previously. We have used the principles in this book ourselves with great success, and have taught them to hundreds of other couples in workshops and seminars over the past ten years. We know they work. But we want to be clear right now that ours is not a "sweetness and light" approach. It's about digging deep into your inner self—sometimes into places that are very uncomfortable to visit—and discovering the real source of your difficulties in an intimate relationship. Doing that, and then making the changes we suggest, won't be easy. But the time you spend mastering and applying the concepts we present will pay off in increased intimacy for years to come.

*For the sake of simplicity, we use the term *second marriage* to mean any marriage after the first. Please translate it to whatever number actually describes your situation.

We began working together in a private practice with individuals in 1986. We soon discovered we liked to work fast, go deep, and not waste therapeutic dollars. That led us to develop a therapeutic style that was very direct and went straight to the difficult realities. After our marriage in 1988, our interest in couples' work naturally heightened, and we applied those same precepts to that area. A couple of years later, when we expanded into group work and residential retreats, our "cut to the chase" approach quite naturally came along with us.

We began exploring these approaches to relating in our first book, *Dancing in the Dark: The Shadow Side of Intimate Relationships* (North Star Publications, 1994). In that book we examined certain patterns of behavior that all relationships get stuck in from time to time. We included descriptions of the so-called "dark sides" of both partners in various situations that typically arise in relationships. We know from feedback we have received since its publication that those descriptions were so vivid and so compelling that partners couldn't help seeing themselves and their contributions as individuals to the difficult times. We also heard that once partners see themselves more clearly, they are much more willing to take responsibility. If you are not already acquainted with confronting and resolving dark-side material, we suggest you pick up that book.

Sometimes we are asked why we like to work with material that highlights the difficult parts of a relationship and the difficult parts of the partners who comprise it? Aren't things arduous enough already? Don't we just want to get past all that? Our view is that hiding from difficulties just leads to more difficulties, whereas facing them head-on ultimately leads to greater awareness and relief. Greater awareness leads to excitement, which eventually leads to a more fulfilling life.

What You Will Find in This Book

Our work is based on several fundamentals: attention to making a conscious commitment, attention to locating, expressing, and receiving feelings, and attention to talk and touch. We will explore these issues in depth.

The chapters in Part 1, The Second Time Around, explore the nature of conscious commitment. How can you avoid the same mistakes you made the first time? What can you do to ensure a firm foundation in your second marriage? In Part 2, Passion Training: A Passionate Marriage Means Owning Your Feelings, we enter the challenging realm of feelings training. Are you primarily a Thinking type or a Feelings Type? How does this play out in your relationship? Do you know how to deal effectively with anger in your marriage? How can husbands and wives get unstuck from narrow roles and work together toward wholeness? Part 3, Issues of the Second Marriage: Exes, Children, and Money, addresses issues particular to second marriages: Is an ex-spouse a phantom partner in your current marriage? What are the ins and outs of dealing with your spouse's children? How can you put your relationship with your new partner before that with your child? And how will you deal with the many issues involving making and spending money together? Part 4, Relationship Fitness, explores the following questions. Do you understand the importance of talk and touch in your relationship? Are you and your partner operating from your true selves in your marriage, or are you covering over the difficulties and hoping not to look at them? Finally, we leave you with a word about priorities.

In this, a book on second marriages, we believe partners are more ready for direct and responsible language. Because they have more life-experience under their belts, we make the assumption that partners have an even greater desire for growth and expanding awareness, which if you haven't guessed it already, will be a recurrent theme here. Our assumption is that people who have been through at least one marriage (and that includes ourselves) are getting on in life and don't want to waste time soft-pedaling around tender issues.

You may sometimes observe that we like to exaggerate to get the point across. Sometimes we take one dimension of a person in a case example and only work with that dimension.

For instance, when we talk about men acting from their rational intellect and lacking awareness of their feelings, we don't mean to suggest that *all* men fail *all the time* to know their feeling nature. We are simply drawing attention to an important problem. In fact, we hold that each and every person on the planet is fully multidimensional and that no one person can be narrowed into a single category. However, we all get stuck in certain areas of our lives, and narrowing things into easily visible categories, even starkly obvious ones, can be a helpful device for understanding how to get unstuck.

Joy Happens *after* the Challenge

Some teachers who deal with relationship issues have a tendency to ignore the hard parts in favor of "going only for joy," or some such catch phrase. It is a message that sells over the short term—we would all like to have joy without having to work very hard at it. But from what we've seen, this type of work just doesn't lead to significant lasting change in the real world of intimate relationships. Why? Because partners are not encouraged to learn more about who they are as individuals or who they are together. We take a rather different perspective: Joy is a feeling that happens when we can know and celebrate *all* of who we are, light and dark.

Most of us (as dedicated students of intimacy) have a basic desire to function at a higher level with our intimates and thus are willing to work with our challenging aspects once they are out in the open. The problem is that we cannot make any authentic, lasting changes until we arrive at an understanding of where *we* are, warts and all. We need to see ourselves in a truthful light, even if doing so may not be enhancing to our ego. And that's one of the key messages of this book: *We must learn to become aware of what we are unaware of, to become conscious of what we don't know about ourselves.*

Our culture, as a whole, wants to hide from difficulty, preferring to envision fairy-tale outcomes. The net result is that people are ill-equipped when it comes to slogging through the challenging parts of intimacy—the parts that arise in each and every relationship where truth is being told, or needs to be told. We tend to run away, withdraw emotionally, try to change the other person, become defensive, counterattack—or do anything other than stopping and taking a look inside. But in order to go into the richness of intimate relating, we *must* go beyond these childish strategies and learn to consistently make the effort to search inward.

We regard it as given that love and kisses and tenderness and appreciation are wonderful and necessary aspects of juicy intimate relating, but we don't write much about those things, largely because they are well-covered by others. Also, in our experience, if a couple tries to make love and kisses the mainstay of their relationship when they are not dealing with feelings of anger and resentment, they eventually get stagnation and sourness, whether they like it or not. On the other hand, a couple who is willing to work directly with the anger, resentment, stagnation, and sourness that rise up in their relationship from time to time *end up automatically* with love and kisses when the difficult feelings are cleared up.

PART 1

The Second Time Around

1

Avoiding the Same Mistakes

After one or more failed marriages, most of us want the answer to this fundamental question: "How can I avoid the same mistakes, the same problems that occurred in my last marriage?" Sadly, the most common answer is: "I'll marry a different person this time!" But we are living in an illusion if we think we can leave a failed marriage and make an immediate leap to a significantly higher-functioning second marriage without first addressing one of the major causes of the initial breakdown—ourselves!

The truth is marriages break down because both partners have difficult aspects and don't have the wherewithal to deal with the problems when they arise. For example, we have the controller, who always needs to be right, and the victim, who always manages to blame the other person. After the commitment is made, a whole tribe of inner children emerges: the egocentric child, who only wants to focus on self; the collapsed child, who gives up too easily; the defiant child, who always says no; the frightened child, who runs for cover behind a defensive wall; and the child in search of effortless, everlasting harmony with a good mommy or daddy. We see the person who can't receive from the other; the overly controlling intellectualizer who can't

3

recognize feelings; and the out-of-control feelings-based person who doesn't know how to set or respect boundaries.

Moseley's Law of Attraction

We have learned from our own experience, and from participants in our workshops and seminars over the past ten years, what we regard as one of the basic laws of intimate relationships. We call it Moseley's Law of Attraction: *We are attracted to partners who are about equally matched with us in terms of emotional maturity.* This means that a partner who has unresolved wounds will attract someone equally wounded (even though it might not be evident at first). A partner who is blocked in one area attracts someone who has a corresponding block. A partner who is underdeveloped in some significant way eventually discovers that he or she is attracted to someone who needs to grow about the same amount or in the same way. Of course none of this is evident at the beginning!

This law of attraction leads to situations that are annoying, to be sure, but it is perfectly formulated for personal growth. Recognition of this law leads to an important conclusion: If we truly desire to avoid the same mistakes we made before in love, we can—and must—change *ourselves.* If we want a more aware partner, we must undertake to know ourselves better. If we want to attract a more mature masculine or feminine partner, we must become that ourselves. If we desire more aliveness in others, we must be willing to become more responsible for our own aliveness, for who we are and what we create around us.

Don't Avoid Yourself

Here's the corollary to the law of attraction: *If you want to avoid mistakes in intimacy, don't avoid yourself.* Second marriages that start off with greater ease and higher functioning seem to share four common characteristics:

- Partners are determined to learn about *discovering and expressing their own wants and needs.*

- They are more willing *to get honest about personal values* early on.
- They make the effort *to learn more about what their partner needs* (and also how to go about satisfying those needs).
- They engage in *some concentrated endeavor to heal themselves before leaping again.*

Let's take a closer look.

Find and Express Your Own Wants and Needs

Try to answer these questions: What are your primary needs in your relationship? What are the two or three things you really need from your mate in order to stay healthy and happy in your marriage? What do you need to keep fueled up so you can carry on in life in the most alive way? What specific things could your partner do to bring about the fulfillment of those needs?

These may seem like simple questions, but (as you probably discovered) most people have to struggle for clean, clear, and honest answers. And that's a big problem. If you can't articulate your own needs, how can you expect your partner to know what they are? If your partner doesn't know what they are, how can they be met?

We can remember our own struggles with articulating needs in our first days together. Doug was still feeling the effects of years of touch deprivation in his first marriage. He had become very clear that he wasn't willing to commit again to any new relationship without daily touch being part of it. However, knowing that and saying it out loud were two different things. It felt like a big risk to make a demand so early and risk losing the love of his life, but he took a breath and went ahead. Naomi was a little taken aback by such a forthright demand so early in the relationship, but she agreed to have a go at it. Then it was her turn to express her needs. Naomi had experienced fourteen years of disappointment and a betrayal in her first marriage, so honesty and fidelity were at the top of her needs list. We had already agreed to honesty, and now she declared that betrayal on Doug's part meant she was out.

Doug also needed a regular time to pursue his personal studies, which began when his first marriage ended. Naomi needed time together with Doug and focused attention from him. She needed regular, meaningful talk and she needed to be listened to.

Even though it took a stretch for both of us, with these needs out in the open, clearly articulated, we set a foundation that still holds up our marriage.

In our first marriages, neither of us had enough courage or experience to express our needs clearly and directly. We were determined not to make that mistake again. In our work, we have noticed that this attitude also seems to be present in other second marriages that get off to good beginnings. Clearly, *the sooner you both express and define your needs, the better*. Partners in second marriages simply can't afford to ignore or deny what is important to them and pretend it doesn't matter.

Be Honest about Your Values

If you and your partner are not open and honest about your values in the beginning, you're in for trouble later. When it comes to values, people tend to assume everything will turn out okay because "we love each other." But the truth is seldom so benign. When it comes to values, the big four are sex, money, children, and spiritual beliefs. After that come a whole range of career and personal issues, big and little, that need to be discussed.

Sex Partners entering second marriages who are not in harmony around sexual relating are waving a big red flag. Sex is a big part of the glue that helps a couple to stay together and enrich each other. When sex is not satisfying early on, it's a sign that important issues, perhaps having nothing to do with sex, are not being addressed.

Money Money concerns also need to be explored thoroughly. Who's earning it now? Who's going to be making it? Does one partner secretly expect to be able to quit working? How will you combine your incomes? How will you share spending responsibilities? How will you deal with personal wealth accumulated before the relationship started? How much will you spend on children from previous marriages? How will you agree on what those expenses will be? What about past debts? What about budgets? Savings goals? Clarifying these issues may seem like an obvious thing to do, but it's easy to want to hide from the harder realities during the romantic stages.

Children It is the rare partner in a second marriage who is prepared for the challenges and complexities of coparenting a blended family. Complex custody agreements, visitation schedules, wounded and sometimes hostile ex-spouses, wounded and sometimes hostile children, difficulties with trust and fragile new commitments, leftover feelings, egos galore, and much more—including the new couple having a child together—can upset the delicate balance of a new second marriage. Finding adaptive ways to blend families requires two partners who are on top of things. It is not for the faint of heart! The more understandings you can work out ahead of time, the better chance a partnership has of thriving.

Spiritual Beliefs In our homogenizing culture, differing spiritual backgrounds do not appear to be the same hurdle they were historically, but early in the relationship, each individual needs to develop a clear vision about where the other stands. Differences that seem easily surmountable in the romantic stage can easily turn into major stumbling blocks later.

Career and Personal Issues Most newly developing couples make a fair effort to discuss career *versus* home life, along with relationship goals, but have a tendency to overlook those issues that seem small at first but very often can turn into big issues over time. For example, who will do the cooking? How are household tasks going to be handled? Who will clean the house? What about childcare, carpools, grocery shopping, bill paying, allocation of space inside the house, and so forth?

When partners become stressed and pressed for time, as they invariably will, these issues gain in prominence.

In first marriages, especially at the beginning, partners usually don't want to seem overly controlling. Fear of rejection is high, so many feelings are not articulated. Fairy-tale expectations mean that both partners make unfounded assumptions—of course he'll help with the housework; of course she won't mind if I spend time with the guys. In a second marriage, you must ask yourself if you'd rather find these things out sooner or later. Getting those rose-colored glasses off early leads to a smoother relationship over the long haul.

Learn More about Your Partner's Needs

Acknowledging he is from Mars and she is from Venus is a good beginning, but what will you do about living with those differences? Partners need to regularly set aside the time to ask about each other's needs and keep themselves updated about whether these needs are, in fact, being met. Here is an area where listening skills are particularly important: after each partner expresses their needs, try repeating back what has been heard until the expresser is fully satisfied their message has been received. Sometimes a need can't or won't be met by a partner and it's better to have that out in the open rather than try to hide from it.

Heal Yourself First

Too many people plunge right into a second marriage before the dust has settled on their first one. Even though they lost themselves in their first marriage, they con themselves into believing it won't happen again. All kinds of business with the ex-spouse and children has been left unfinished. They are still blaming the past and their spouse for their failures in love. These people had better hope the angels have been doing a lot of work for them in the meantime, because they themselves certainly haven't.

When you step right out of one marriage into the next without taking a breath, there is a great possibility that part of you is desperately seeking a "mommy" or "daddy" to replace the one you have just lost. And the faster the better, so the new mommy or daddy can help you hide from the grief and pain of losing the first one. The rescuing partner who hooks up with this kind of "leaper" is often inordinately hungry. In clearer moments, the rescuer knows that the leaper needs to have more alone time to get a new bearing on life. But rescuers are so afraid of losing the other, they often go against their own better judgment and become too involved too quickly.

In the beginning, it's a great match: hungry meets hungry. That's no problem during the initial romance, but troubles always emerge later on. When you leap too fast, you don't get a chance to dissolve or resolve your bond with your previous partner. With old bonds still in place, there just isn't enough space for the new partner. As time goes by, the new partner comes to resent being the substitute mommy or daddy. Many times, the leaper uses the new partner—consciously or unconsciously—to take away the pain of a difficult parting; then, when the leaper is recovered, the rescuer is cast aside. The problems are too many to count and the troubles that eventually emerge are likely to be more difficult than the troubles that were avoided by moving so fast. Deep down, we all know that in the long run it will be more advantageous to concentrate on building a new self *between* relationships. Unfortunately, this is an area where many of us go blind.

We are all hungry for love. How much better things would be if we could only remember that a match in intimacy goes a lot farther when "fuller" meets "fuller." How do you get fuller? By facing the pain and grief of previous failures. By getting to know who you are without a partner. By allowing and knowing your hunger without having to race to fill it. By taking your time. By realistically assessing yourself. By taking responsibility for yourself in the world. By consciously putting aside old intimate ties.

The truth is, nobody really wants to do this type of heavy work. But those who don't will eventually end up repeating at least some of the dysfunctional dramas from a previous marriage. Those who insist on blaming their exes for failures in intimacy are usually in for a rude awakening once they settle into a second marriage. In fact, a few people have to go through this process many times before they wake up to the one constant in their failed marriages: themselves.

It Takes Two to Tangle

Intimate partners might be quick to identify the difficulties in each other, but usually are slower to look inside of themselves to uncover their own negative contribution. Every less-than-satisfying interaction we've ever witnessed has required two participants, and when we get right down to it, we discover both are pretty close to equal in dysfunction! But in stuck marriages, partners steadfastly refuse to explore their own responsibility, preferring instead to point the finger at the other.

None of us is inherently "good" or "bad" or "healthy" or "dysfunctional." We can all be loving and caring *and* we can all be difficult. And we will be all of these things in relationship to another. By midlife, most of us have done a reasonably solid inventory of the parts of ourselves that are enhancing to the self-image we want to hold. And why not? Those parts are comparatively easy to come to terms with. It is another story with the parts that are not enhancing to our self-image: the emotionally young parts; the defensive parts; the controlling parts; the puffed-up parts; the rejecting parts; the self-absorbed parts that expect a lot and are too busy to give much. Our egos would like to think we could fool everyone into believing we don't have these parts (perhaps fool ourselves, too), but life doesn't work that way. We can't surgically remove or deny the aspects of ourselves that get in the way of intimate relating. In intimacy, all parts of ourselves get smoked out. An intimate relationship is the one place we cannot hide.

When we are blind to our own difficult parts, we are blind to our role in the problems that come up in our interpersonal experiences. Most of us have spent a lifetime avoiding and distancing ourselves from our unflattering and distasteful inner aspects. Across our entire culture, we are encouraged to look outside of ourselves for someone to blame when things go wrong. Some of us are so focused outside of ourselves that we are seriously underdeveloped when it comes to tracking what we, ourselves, are even feeling. At the same time, while we may be relatively blind to our own sore spots, we are adept at putting our partner's issues in the spotlight. We hope that when you have finished reading our book, you will begin to understand the important role of self-awareness and responsibility in marriage.

The tasks we've outlined in this chapter may sound like a lot to deal with, but it's not that difficult if partners *start early and keep on top of problems*. In our first marriage, we have a hard time seeing problematic patterns because we only have one experience to go by. In a subsequent marriage, we have the great advantage of experience and the maturity that goes along with it. When you see old patterns emerging again, or numbness setting in, or dysfunctional inner characters popping up to get in the way of joy in intimacy, use it as a wake-up call to live this new marriage with awareness.

2

Conscious Commitment

Until one is committed, there is hesitancy, the chance to draw back, always ineffectiveness, concerning all acts of initiative (and creation). There is one elementary truth, the ignorance of which kills countless ideas and splendid plans: That the moment one definitely commits oneself, then providence moves too. All sorts of things occur to help one that would never otherwise have occurred. A whole stream of events issues from the decision, raising in one's favor all manner of unforeseen incidents and meetings and material assistance which no man could have dreamed would have come his way. Whatever you can do, or dream you can, begin it. Boldness has genius, power, and magic in it. Begin it now.

GOETHE

Here's a situation we frequently see in our couples therapy practice. Both partners come in saying that they want to make their relationship all it can be. When we get past the first layers of whatever is going on in their relationship, however, it becomes evident one or both partners have a foot (or at least a toe) out the door of the relationship. In some cases partners aren't fully committed to each other after many years of marriage. When such a couple says they want to iron out the difficulties they experience in their everyday lives, they are essentially asking for Band-Aids to stop a hemorrhage.

Such a superficial approach to a relationship is a waste of time. It might look good for a while, but the bleeding will always start again. We want partners to grow, allow deep vulnerability, and make leaps in their ability to relate to each other. This kind of work takes two people who have established a foundation and are determined to stick it out when the going gets tough. *In order to make lasting changes, a wobbling couple needs an ironclad both-feet-in commitment to remain together for at least six months (one year is even better), along with a determination to work on themselves and their relationship during that time.*

Partners who have been through one or more marriages like to think they've been through the fire, and they know what commitment is all about. But it's important to remember this fact: They weren't able to commit to a relationship in the past and, in our experience, commitment is an even bigger decision the second time around. Eyes are more open. Time is more precious. Scars remain from past pain. Our protective instincts are on full alert. The beginning of a relationship, then, is the perfect time to explore what deep commitment really means.

Commitment: The Basics

What does commitment mean? The quote from Goethe that begins this chapter says it as well as anything we've ever seen. *We regard commitment to a relationship as a pledge to bring all of oneself and all of one's truth into a mutually defined and sexually monogamous experience with another person.* While that definition covers part of it, commitment is even more complicated. In the realm of intimate relationship, commitment is both an end result *and* an ongoing process. It is made once but needs to be renegotiated as a relationship evolves. It is one of life's most important decisions, and it doesn't really mean anything without follow through every day.

Can you have a committed relationship without marriage? For a period of time perhaps—but ultimately, no. A half-committed relationship is actually a noncommitted relationship in which two people are testing each other. When a couple says they are committed but won't marry, at least one partner is holding back. When intimates are holding back from each other, full potential for healing, growth, and love simply can't be achieved.

The diehard noncommitter is usually able to philosophize eloquently about the irrelevancy of committing; but despite this intellectualizing, that person can never know about the alchemy that occurs when a commitment *is* made. Once partners make a commitment to each other, it opens up a whole new realm of possibilities. Refusing to commit, on the other hand, eventually leaves a relationship stalled. An intimate relationship is a living organism. In order to keep it alive, the partners must keep it growing. A refusal to move past a stalled point leaves a relationship stuck. In the world of intimate relating, sticking at one point too long leads to decay.

The stories we hear from individuals who hold back from full commitment are similar. Some partners have a deep fear they will "lose their soul" if they commit. Other partners fear being "used" or taken advantage of. Many harbor the secret (or perhaps not so secret) fantasy that someone "better" (more attractive, less controlling, more financially stable, more mature, less defensive, more sexy, less angry, and so forth) will come along if they just hold out (that is: withhold) long enough. They keep their partner tied down to meet their own security needs, while they attempt to keep their options as open as possible.

All noncommitters will eventually face a decision. If they want to experience more aliveness in the relationship part of their lives, they must decide to move to a deeper level of involvement—or they must cut loose and start off in another direction. As we will see, a refusal to take either one of these challenges will only result in gradual deadening.

Why Is Commitment So Vital?

Commitment is a co-created boundary around a relationship. It gives definition and testimony that participants are dedicated to a long-term course of action. It provides a foundation that supports the development of two individuals and their capacity to learn about love and all of life's feelings. It is a place of refuge, a place where partners can let go—allowing imperfections, allowing vulnerability, nourishing and being nourished. It offers one of the few real opportunities we'll ever get to experience being accepted for all of who we are and to learn to accept others for all of who they are. It provides a crucible in which two individuals can meld and grow together into greater consciousness—or a prison where, day after day, partners coexist, reminded of their failure to grow. Either way, commitment serves to help us become more aware.

These days, a lot of people don't want boundaries (teachers who claim that "you can have it all without personal limitation" have no problem finding students who want to buy their message). The problem is, after the romantic stage is over, deeper love, acceptance, and all the rest of it can't really happen when one partner is ready to exit the minute things don't go according to his or her fantasy of how things should be. Without a sincere commitment, opportunism, fantasies, power games, and self-defense gradually take over and eventually destroy the relationship.

We have nothing against two souls coming together to meet mutual needs. Yet we have seen that when friends/lovers "just get together," it is often based on needs for security and comfort. It is convenient for the moment and might even be healing for both in the short run, but sooner or later the partners will come up against the "commit or quit" decision. Before a commitment, partners can play at relationship like children: neither has to take responsibility or compromise or shift to any significant degree. The real movement toward mature adulthood begins when the first commitment is made, when they finally make a decision to jump in and *stay in*. *The presence of an external boundary requires partners to begin learning to go inside.*

Ironically, the most problematic behavior patterns emerge in full force only *after* a commitment has been made. Now that may be bad news to those who are looking for angels and bottomless wells of unconditional love; but when we understand that difficult patterns of behavior are *always* going to emerge in *every* relationship, the situation looks a little different. The difficult patterns are not there to cause us misery; they are there to challenge us to become more aware. The question is finally not merely whether to commit or not, but whether we want to take on life at its fullest, rise to meet the challenges it has to offer, and harvest the potential rewards—or stay asleep.

Gail and Joel: Struggling with Commitment

Gail and Joel are in their mid-thirties and have been going together for almost two years. Right now, they are struggling with commitment. Gail was married briefly in her early twenties— during a faint, she quipped. Joel was married for ten years and got through his divorce about three years ago. From his brief description, it was clear his marriage left him with some scars. Neither has any children.

The first year was a wonderful time for both of them. In the last couple of months, however, things haven't been going as well. Both have been edgy, overreacting to each other and having too many circular, out-of-proportion fights over issues that are not really important to either of them. They decided to get to the bottom of what was going on and came to us for help.

Since we don't like to waste time, and since Gail and Joel fit our profile of a couple with commitment difficulties, we went right to the heart of the issue: "What is your commitment to this relationship?" Both looked a little dumbfounded. They responded that they had no particular commitment, but they cared a great deal for each other and didn't have intimate involvements with any other people. They planned on continuing to see each other—and that was as far as it went. As the session progressed, we began to iron out some of the surface issues presented to us, but we didn't feel as if we had gotten to the core of the problem.

At the next session, Gail came forward. She had been thinking some more about the commitment question. Her first marriage hadn't worked out, and she had learned that the commitment hadn't really meant anything. Since the divorce she had been independent for a number of years, had proven she could get along perfectly well on her own, and didn't really need a commitment now. She wanted to impress on us that she didn't fit that trite mold of the stereotyped female, hungry to catch a man.

"Oh, so you don't want a commitment, then?" we asked. Well, that wasn't exactly true either. She was confused.

Joel was listening while Gail talked, and we asked what was going on with him. He reported that he had thought a little about commitment in the preceding months, but felt it was still too early. It had taken him a long time to get out of his first marriage, and he was in no hurry to leap in again. Gail knew he cared for her—he made sure of that. They had good times together and good sex. He also had space enough to see his friends and time enough to do the things he liked to do alone. If Gail could just get over this moodiness she had been going through lately, everything would be perfect—again.

What's Going On?

What's going on here underneath it all? Gail wants a commitment but is afraid to bring the matter out in the open—even to herself. A big part of her wishes Joel would seize the initiative and make it perfectly clear that he wants her and only her. If she were to push for a commitment or even bring up the subject, it would put her in control and she doesn't want that. Maybe he doesn't feel strongly enough about her to commit, which means she would have to face rejection. She doesn't want that, either. Nevertheless, she has a strong sense that a commitment would bring them both to an even deeper love. In addition, she would like to have a child with him—and her biological clock is counting down. All this and much more is swirling around inside her—and she can't really get to any of it until the commitment question comes out into the open. She feels blocked and she can't hide it anymore.

Joel would rather keep things the way they have been. Up to this point, he has been able to go in and out of his "cave" pretty much as he likes. Commitment is something "out there" somewhere, but he feels no rush to address it. And besides, why stir up all those messy, volatile feelings? Joel doesn't really want any boundaries other than the informal ones that have evolved. He has no interest in adding more definition to their relationship. Nothing is wrong with his position; but in the context of an evolving intimate relationship, its shortcomings are apparent.

Men, Women, and Commitment

Joel and Gail are up against a very basic male-female difference that we see over and over again in our private and group work. Whenever we ask a woman what her needs in relationship are, at the top of the list is *commitment from her partner.* She needs boundary and definition. As her love deepens, this need for definition becomes even more important. Boundaries in her intimate world don't fence her in; they give her freedom to be more of who she is, and she naturally assumes that her partner should feel the same way. We could speculate that this need stems from a very deep, instinctual drive for genetic survival, for her to have a place to bear and nurture children, but figuring out why doesn't really matter. What matters is that, for the majority of women, the need is present and powerful. It's not trivial, arbitrary, or likely to change. It just is.

Men may make note of their desire for sexual exclusivity, but commitment (with all of the boundaries and restrictions that are attached to it) is not the need they are likely to mention first. Typically, when we ask a man what his needs are in a relationship, high on the list is his need to be deeply accepted, or received, by his partner. He needs to be accepted for who he is, and being deeply received sexually is usually a big part of that.

During the romantic phase, this essential difference between men and women is not usually noticeable. Both partners feel that their primary needs are being met. Both feel received and accepted. He gives and she gives. Boundaries are irrelevant because all there is for each partner is the other. As time goes by, however, things change—especially for her. She begins to feel the need for another layer of commitment.

Why is this so?

Typically, as the relationship gets more serious, in order to experience her essential feminine nature, a woman instinctively wants to go to a place of surrender and openness with her partner. She wants a deeper form of love, and that requires increased vulnerability. Since this is something the man wants from her as well, all is still in harmony. But opening emotionally to this degree means shedding lifelong defenses, and this does not happen automatically. Before she can feel safe surrendering deeply, a woman feels an expanding need for containment. She feels, in a word, an increasing urge for *commitment*.

For a man, the need for commitment and containment often doesn't follow as naturally. When he's not in the heat of passion, his mind tends to dominate his body. Rational minds must wrestle long and hard with the concept of giving up huge amounts of spontaneous freedom in order to go deeper with one woman. Just as a man wants a woman to give from her deepest place, he wants to give *to* her from his deepest place; but men and women tend to give in different ways.

The man's urge is to push to get inside, and not just sexually. Yes, the man needs to give of himself, *but he has an even deeper need to have his being, his essence, accepted and received by a woman.* Receiving is not foremost for him. He doesn't know what it's like to have someone needing to push inside him and connect directly to his heart. Later, if he gets past this hurdle of the first commitment, we can almost bet that he will experience *her* pushing just as hard to get inside *him*—to his feelings. At that point, he will get a chance to recognize how much vulnerability is required for him to open to her (and how scary it can be), but we are jumping ahead of our story. For now, in these early stages, he needs acceptance, and doesn't really feel the need for commitment the same way a woman does. That's just how he is.

So here's the situation. She wants to go deeper into love, deeper into her receptive feminine nature, and to do that she needs a greater commitment. She wants to move the relationship along. He wants her openness and acceptance, but commitment means boundaries—and creating boundaries for himself is not first on his list of priorities. Extend this a little farther and she is saying she wants to *keep on* growing and needs *more* commitment in order to do that. In the intimate realms, he tends to prefer the status quo: If it ain't broke, don't fix it. He would rather have time to accumulate more data— "Let me think about this."

So how are Joel and Gail progressing? Gail has achieved more clarity and is willing to express herself: She wants a deeper commitment. That's an essential need for her. She feels great vulnerability expressing this need, but she can't hold back from her truth now that her awareness is developing. Now Joel must respond. If he refuses to respond, she won't be able to explore this essential matter and she will begin to feel blocked. If one partner is stuck, the relationship ultimately becomes stuck. Her need may not be met, but she wants to know what's going on. She wants to know one way or the other, so *she* can make a decision. If he meets her need, they move forward. If he refuses to commit, she will have to sacrifice an essential need of hers or the entire relationship.

A Refusal to Commit Means "You're Not Good Enough"

There is a lot more going on here than male-female differences. First, Gail's position. As Gail risks putting her needs out into the open, she begins to realize that, underneath it all, she fears Joel is secretly still on the lookout for someone better. As he holds back from committing, she hears, "You're not good enough for me," and feels the need to hold back herself as well. And, to be honest, some of what she is sensing about him is true.

Beneath a refusal to commit after a lengthy time together is an implicit statement that the partner is not good enough to commit to. Many a partner who is holding back from making a commitment will want to put more flowery words around it, but cut them away and "not good enough" is the message. If the commitment issue does not get resolved, then, this couple is clearly heading for a split.

Joel believes he has a good reason to be cautious about commitment—his first marriage turned out to be a mess. But the fact remains that he is holding back, which essentially means he is conveying that Gail isn't good enough to commit to. Now that Gail's wish for a commitment is out in the open, something else becomes more evident: The invisible relationship scales are tipped in his favor. By refusing to commit, he implicitly holds a more special or "better-than" position, while Gail (in this particular territory) holds a "less-than" position.

The partner holding the "better than" position is generally fairly comfortable with the arrangement, for obvious reasons. It is a safe position and he (usually "he," but of course that is not always the case) is probably getting his basic needs met for the moment. The partner who wants more commitment eventually ends up feeling like she (usually "she") is being given crumbs. So Gail feels "less-than" and controlled. She feels a deep desire to move this situation to a place in which the power is more balanced.

Couples in this circumstance can carry on satisfactorily from day to day, and their relationship may be functional in many different ways. But inevitably the "less-than" partner begins to feel angry. Ultimately, that partner will punish or withhold from the partner who refuses to commit. Gail is approaching that point.

Joel, however, doesn't see himself as holding a "better-than" position relative to Gail. He cares deeply for her and, as far as he is concerned, things are just the way they ought to be. He doesn't see that he has any special control, but he does sense he would *lose* control if things were to go as Gail wishes.

As Gail begins to express her demands, he thinks, "Why should it be her way? Isn't this some kind of trade-off, where she gets what she wants and I lose?" One thing is clear: With one failed marriage under his belt, he doesn't want to commit again unless he is with a woman he *knows* will be able to receive and accept him on the deepest levels and not turn into the cold, distant woman his first wife did. And he *doesn't* know that yet, so why should he commit? In fact, as Gail begins to press him, he feels less accepted and begins to pull away slightly.

A trend is clearly starting to develop in this relationship. Gail is not getting what she needs and is beginning to pull back and withhold. Joel, sensing Gail's withholding, also begins to withhold. Withholding in one partner ultimately leads to even more withholding in the other. Unless a big shift takes place, the writing is on the wall for these two. And there's more to uncover.

Murky Power Struggles

In the weeks before Gail began to express her need for a commitment, she and Joel found themselves overreacting to each other and fighting with intensity that was clearly out of proportion to the relatively minor issues involved. Why?

As we've seen, the partner who wants more commitment is automatically in a "less-than" position. She (for the sake of this discussion) doesn't want to keep hammering away at it—after all, to be seen as *begging* a partner for a commitment is not very ego-enhancing; in fact, it's painful. So she buries those "less-than" feelings of hurt and anger and continues as if everything is fine. But there is always a consequence.

When a partner is feeling angry and hurt beneath the surface, these feelings can manifest as an attitude of contentiousness and defensiveness. In her underdog position, she has an extra need to assert herself, prove herself, get respect, and prop up her self-image in the relationship.

The net result is that murky, pervasive power struggles often get played out over relatively obscure issues, issues that have no apparent relation to commitment. Neither person is conscious of how the commitment issue has been deflected into other territory, and thus they scratch their heads about why they are struggling with each other. Everything becomes confusing and frustrating. But one thing is certain: Both partners become aware that the relationship is not feeding them as much as they want it to. In fact, the opposite seems to be taking place: A great deal of the energy seems to get used up in the relationship, and both partners feel drained.

If the matter of the underlying commitment is not addressed soon, these murky power struggles and habits of relating get entrenched and become very difficult to break later on (witness a bickering middle-aged couple). The relationship gradually spirals downward. Even the partner who originally wanted a deeper commitment begins to wonder why on earth she or he would want to commit to such an unnurturing situation. We have seen more than a few relationships where the partner who desired more commitment eventually lost interest, and suddenly the withholder was sparked to commit, only to discover it was too late to turn things around. What's going on with the noncommitter?

What the Noncommitting Partner Fears

Individuals who enter a relationship but refuse to commit often have an underlying feeling of powerlessness in relation to their mates (and probably in relation to the opposite sex in general). Because they don't really want to know about these feelings of powerlessness (and would probably deny them vigorously), they would much rather set themselves up quietly in the role of "more special" and "better-than." The truth is that withholding commitment is their one strong position. Were they to commit, they would risk losing whatever feelings of power they do have in relation to their partner.

By withholding what a partner strongly wants, they do indeed maintain a position of power in the relationship, even though it is a seducer's kind of power—which is to say, a child's power. Keeping one foot out the door serves to keep the partner off balance, weakened, dancing on eggshells, holding back any dark or threatening feelings.

This makes for a rather unfulfilling drama. Every time the topic comes up, the noncommitting partner dodges, frequently bringing forth all manner of rational explanations about why not to commit. "What is commitment anyway? Who needs it?

We already love each other, so why do I need to prove it? It's only a piece of paper. These days, when things are moving so quickly, how can a person commit to a lifetime? Enlightened people don't have to be concerned with such mundane issues. We're better off as friends. Everyone knows that marriage kills passion, and who wants to ruin what we have?" And so on. The sentiments underneath, however, are quite different: "You might not be good enough for me. I might be swallowed up by you. I feel powerless relative to you." But these words are seldom voiced out loud. In fact, most of the time they are not even allowed to surface in the conscious awareness of the person who is saying them.

Every big knot in relationship requires a significant effort to resolve successfully. That Joel and Gail are not aware of the hidden dynamics of the relationship is not a matter of conscious deception or stupidity. It is simply this: There are things they don't know about themselves, and they need to know those things if they are going to become more developed and more fully present human beings. Getting stuck around commitment is a cue to lead them to discover even more. If their relationship is truly substantial, doing this work of exploration and learning what needs to be learned will untie the knot and allow them to move on.

Hiding behind the Judge

How do people who secretly feel powerless and inadequate stay unaware of and above those feelings? One way is to develop a very powerful "Inner Judge" who harshly evaluates and criticizes everyone and everything. In the daily life of a person who is not in a relationship, that Judge might not be too visible; but when a relationship enters the picture, the Judge comes out in full force—especially as the relationship becomes more serious and intimate.

Rather than risk feeling what is going on underneath the surface, the Judge focuses on finding fault with the partner. When Joel's Judge came out, all he could see were the difficulties *Gail* created by making these demands, the chaotic mess caused by *her*, the child *she* is.

Unfortunately, Judges have great difficulty seeing *themselves* in any kind of clear light. All sight is directed from the "bench" downward. They are so absorbed in the judging process that they are almost entirely unable to grasp that they, themselves, are living in a very tight defensive shell. The greater their feelings of inadequacy and powerlessness, the more strongly this Judge comes out. The more strongly the Judge comes out, the tighter is the defensive shell, and the less available they are to others. It is difficult for anyone to get inside the shell because (in the Judge's eyes) no one is ever good enough. The fantasy love who might be worthy of opening up to never appears—or stays very long. Everyone else eventually leaves, too (actually: gets pushed away) and the delusion is fortified. Of course, no therapist would be worthy enough, either, so seeking help to get through this is almost out of the question.

Joel, however, did try to come to terms with his commitment issues. He has his problems, Gail has her problems—and still he wants her in his life. He sees that her essential needs must be met. He wants his own needs to be met. He is also seeing some of his defenses and fears and he has a desire to grow beyond them. He is getting tired of the seducing game and—surprise!—part of him knows (or suspects) that a commitment will actually be good for him. As he explores himself more deeply, he realizes he never did fully commit to his first marriage—in fact, it was probably part of what led to its breakdown. He is more willing to consider a commitment, but he still wants to come out the other end feeling as if he was true to himself, not being pushed into it.

Clearly, Joel's exploration is not finished yet, and he needs even more information and understanding. But he has taken a huge beginning step. And as we look on at what's happening, we can be amazed along with him to realize that the first time he got married, he didn't even come close to touching any of this understanding about himself. He's just now stumbling into it. So let's hang in there with him and add another couple of pieces to the puzzle.

Commitment Is Painful

Joel's inner fantasy has always been that one day his true and perfect love will arrive—perfect just like him, of course! When he is with this perfect love, there will be no questions in his mind; he will surely be swept away in passion and absolute certainty. All of this sweat, however—all of this pondering, analyzing, and evaluating—does not fit in with his fantasy of how things ought to be. Part of him feels as if something must be wrong, and he sees Gail as the "something wrong."

Here is another place Joel is not seeing clearly. In order to be "swept away," *he* would have to change who *he* is. He is looking for a mythical woman to arrive in his life and do it for him (that is: *to* him). This is not only unrealistic, it is a potentially dangerous way to begin a relationship. Implicitly, he is holding to the fantasy that a decision like this should be easy and painless. He doesn't realize that only the naive child inside of him would believe this.

The cost of committing is high. It means loss of freedom, major increases in responsibility, and a big shift away from the comforts of egocentricity . . . a shift into the need to take account of another person moment by moment for a very long time. *Forever.* It means confronting, dealing with, and possibly defusing the secret specialness he feels—that we all feel—along with uncovering his usually unseen sense of powerlessness. It means a lifetime of struggling through all manner of impossibly complicated issues with a less-than-perfect person, with much less-than-perfect tools. Worse than all that, their relationship might fail in the end, which will lead to even greater possibilities for pain than can be imagined right now. In short, it means dealing with reality.

Listening to Our Conflicting
Inner Voices

Commitment to marriage is a very big decision. Whenever we are up against a major life-decision, our full complexity as human beings comes into play. Instead of hearing one voice that says, "Yes, go for it!" we hear many inner voices—all with something different to say about the decision. Here we have a choice.

First, we can pretend we hear only one clear voice, and plow ahead. That's what a lot of people do in their first marriages. Some people have to get all the way to the divorce proceedings before they recall hearing the inner voice that said it was the wrong move right from the beginning. In his first marriage, Joel didn't listen to his questioning voices. But now he no longer has that option. Failure woke him up.

Our other choice is to listen a little harder. Even though doing so is annoying, laborious, and decidedly unromantic, Joel is now giving himself more space to listen. He is beginning to suspect that only when he hears all the voices clearly can he make a truly conscious commitment.

For example, one of Joel's voices says, "It's too soon; you need more time." Another voice affirms, "She's a great woman, you love her, and the time has come to get serious and go deeper." Yet another voice says, "You need your freedom—no obligations, lots of women." One voice values family and community and sees the importance of evolving as a man. One wants to possess Gail and ravish her; another would prefer a life detached from such mundane hungers. We have seen that a particular shadowy aspect of Joel believes Gail isn't special enough. We can be sure another aspect feels unworthy of her. And on it goes: a huge inner jumble, indeed! If Joel is to be true to himself, he must find some way to contact the majority of these voices—which are just part of himself—and strike a bargain among all of them. And he needs some time now to do this.

Gail has all the same voices and probably a few more. At this moment, her voices appear to present her with less conflict, and we can't argue with her about that. However, our suggestion for her would be that she listen to any doubting voices and deal with them now—because after the commitment, they won't be denied.

Going Deeper

In the case of Gail and Joel and the matter of their commitment, she was clear and he was not. The chances are the partner who is clear about things will wait for a while . . . then close
the door. The partner who is not clear has a lot of wrestling to
do—looking at the issue from all angles, feeling the major ups
and downs, feeling clear one day and not so clear the next. If
he diligently stays with the process, he will probably gain clarity and, because of the work he's putting in, a clarity that will
stick. He might decide to come "in" or he might decide to be
"out." Either way will add to his overall growth and movement.
However, for Gail and Joel that moment of total clarity has not
yet arrived. How can they move their relationship forward
while the search for clarity goes on?

Joel wants to go deeper with Gail but honestly feels that he
cannot make a lifetime commitment right now. Gail appears to
be more ready, although Joel's doubt probably reflects some of
her own questions about the situation as well. (It's not *all* his
problem.) She's also been through a failure and must be feeling
fear about leaping in again. But if they don't make a step toward deeper commitment right now, how will they be able to
go on to discover if each is right for the other?

At this point Joel must either take a leap in faith or bring
something to the table that will come close enough to meeting
Gail's need to keep her in, to keep her working on the relationship with him. Here's what he came up with.

For the next three months, Joel declared, he will bring himself wholeheartedly into the relationship with Gail. That means
sexual fidelity and a commitment to seek and speak the truth
about all of himself, good and bad. He also wants Gail to be
truthful with him in regard to the easy parts and the difficult
parts. In that three-month period, they will both make a determined effort to share all the feelings they are having and go immediately into all issues that arise, just as if they had tied the
knot. They will both seek to find out all they need to know
about each other in order to make a commitment—or not. He

won't hold back any part of himself and he doesn't want her to, either. At the end of three months, they will sit down together and decide whether to recommit or not. Presuming they do decide to recommit at that time, within six months he will propose marriage.

She accepted his idea. It is not everything she wanted, but there is some excitement in it for her. They are moving beyond where they were before. Some boundaries are beginning to take shape. Setting a "deadline" gives her a feeling of safety. She is not just wandering aimlessly, possibly wasting her time. Deep down, she too had doubts about committing, and this will give her more of a chance to come clear as well.

This formal agreement might sound a bit mechanical and unromantic, especially if you are a lucky soul who took the dive and haven't had a doubt ever since. But Gail and Joel are not in that position. They've had plenty of experience with doubts. Her first marriage was more like a blip on the screen, but it alerted her to what can go wrong. Joel's marriage felt like a big mistake to him, one he didn't want to repeat.

The wholehearted, time-bound commitment with a mutually agreed-upon renegotiation point is a good answer for now. If Joel applies himself to the task he has set out for himself, he will become clearer and more able to make a conscious commitment (or not), a commitment that fully takes into account the difficult and painful aspects of this process. In the end, as a result of having worked out this compromise approach, the chances are much higher that his commitment—if he makes it—will come from a deeper place *within himself*, that it will be more of what we call a *conscious commitment*. This is the kind of commitment that will hold and endure.

The Need for a Decision

In the end, all couples have to find their own way through the commitment dilemma. The main requirement is to develop a mutually agreed-on strategy and follow through on it. Couples who do not make an agreement or establish a boundary tend to waffle and wander as the months go by. In our experience, after eighteen months to two years of this, the relationship reaches its limits in terms of healing potential and begins to go downhill. Resentments build, partners relate like brother and sister rather than intimate partners, and eventually the relationship fizzles out. No decision about commitment is ultimately a decision to kill the relationship.

We have made an effort here to lay out many of the more important aspects of commitment because we believe they should be identified and considered anytime that partners are serious about moving their relationship forward. That's the head work and it must be done. Then there is the ineffable part of commitment, the mystery of it, the deep feeling around it, the yearning for it, the eternal drive toward it in people everywhere that can't be captured by any analysis—and that is the voice of the heart.

All people going through the commitment dilemma ultimately have to ask themselves, "Is my heart really in this relationship?" Setting aside all the laundry lists of issues and character traits, we have to ask: *Do I really want this person?* If the answer is "yes," everything else can be worked through—presuming there is a strong desire on both sides to do so.

If you can't get a "yes" from your heart, it probably means that the time has come to move on. Choose the single life and make the best of that for the time being. Then, when you are ready in the future, take a risk, go deeper, and try for the relationship that will really feed you. Just remember: You only get fed in proportion to your ability to feed another person; and in order to be desired by others, you must be able to demonstrate your desire for them.

PART 2

Passion Training: A Passionate Marriage Means Owning Your Feelings

3

The Mind-Body/
Husband-Wife Split
and the Potential
for Wholeness

We all have a Thinking self and a Feelings self within us. Ideally, *both* these parts would be developed and available to us, moment by moment, as required in life. As individuals who were in balance internally we would have our fullest potential available, both as individuals in life and as partners in intimacy. That, as we know, is seldom the case. Most of us have under-developed Feelings selves, and worse yet, have difficulty learning the lessons from the one who really could help us become more whole: our partner.

Thoughts and Feelings

Each of us has a *Thinking* (mental or cerebral) experience of life and a *Feeling* (emotional) experience of life. It is as if we have two selves in one body, both responding and reacting differently to everything that goes on around us. Each of these selves uses language that is not easily comprehended by the other self.

In our culture, the Thinking self tends to dominate and we learn its language best. Most men are already inclined that way; and most women have learned they are better off, in our culture at least, if they get with the mental program. When men and women are asked where their center of awareness is, they both tend to locate it in their heads. Operating primarily from the neck up, we interpret, analyze, synthesize, make judgements, draw from past memories, anticipate future experiences, and generally make intellectual sense of our worlds. And all this is as it should be.

Right alongside our cerebral experience of the world, however, we also have an ongoing feeling experience of the world. Feelings come from our body, and are related to our instincts, our intuition, and our inner knowing. Every stimulus strong enough to engender a thought also engenders a feeling. Just as we have a continuous movement of thoughts, we also have a continuous movement of feelings; and we can become aware of these feelings *if we are willing to learn something about feeling language.*

In an ideal world, well-adjusted people would have both their mental and feeling selves available at any given moment. All individuals would be able to make use of both perception domains, synthesize the information that comes in, and act with the fullest, most comprehensive awareness possible. In a well-adjusted intimate relationship, both partners would have this kind of balance and relate to each other from their thoughts and feelings equally: meaning common sense, problem solving, and constructive planning would co-exist with passion and inner truth. But life doesn't make it that easy for us.

For the majority of people, the Thinking self becomes more developed, so it is usually first to come to our awareness. Being first in line, it has a very strong tendency to take precedence over the Feelings self. In some cases, this dominance is so complete that the feeling experience is barely recognizable. In fact, individuals who are very solidly entrenched in thinking mode might even question whether there even *is* an ongoing feeling experience. To these people, the rational part of themselves is everything; the reality that the head can grasp is the *only* reality; the language of the mental self is the only language. However in thinking they know *all* there is to know, they set the stage for delusion and stuckness—particularly in their intimate lives.

The usual perception is that women have developed their Feelings self while men have developed their Thinking self and that this difference accounts for a big part of the gender struggles. We don't see it being quite as simple as that. Women might have better *access* to their feelings, but sharing them cleanly and clearly is another story. When their defenses are up, women have a tendency to jump to their heads as quickly as the men. One thing does seem clear however: women are much more likely to push for more feelings in their intimate lives.

The Potential for Wholeness

Intimate relationships give us the perfect opportunity to listen to the quiet voice of our less developed self. How? We listen to it speak (if we are willing) through our partner.

Because nature seeks balance (and thus wholeness), one partner is generally more open to exploring feelings than the other. It is a natural combination and if you don't believe it just imagine two hardcore Thinking types living together for years and years: not much problem with feelings because few ever come up! It can be a relationship that works in many ways but it would be numb beyond most people's tolerance. Or how about two Feelings types living together in close quarters for years on end? This relationship creates too much intensity for most people: maybe it is great for those emotional highs, but it would be tough to get much done in the outer world. It works best to have one of each type in the relationship.

When a Thinking person and a Feelings person fall in love, powerful feelings come rushing through. And, for once, neither partner can deny their emotional selves, nor would they want to. All kinds of wonderful sparks fly—and justifiably so. The potential for wholeness and love on both sides is great. After an adjustment period, partners settle down to live together, which gives each the opportunity to learn from the other what needs to be learned.

If each were willing to take the other's strengths, both partners could heal the mind/body split. Thinking partners would take in all they could learn about feelings from the Feelings partner and develop new awareness of the inner world. Feelings people would learn even more about becoming effective in the outer world, a skill that requires some honing of one's rational/analytical side. Both partners would become more balanced as individuals and thus have more possibility for balance as a couple. As balanced individuals in a balanced marriage, they would have a great start on what's required to create a healthy family or undertake whatever mission they have together in the world.

We know the Thinking partner will never become a fully evolved Feelings person, nor would he or she want to be. The same is true for the Feelings type, who has no desire to become a master in the world of rationality. Partners don't have to go all the way, but they *must* demonstrate a sincere willingness to learn from each other and periodically exhibit some evidence that they have received the other's message. It should be a natural: Who doesn't want to become a more balanced, fulfilled, and alive human?

But in reality, a typical relationship often follows this pattern. After the romantic phase, Thinking partners slowly drift back to their habitual way of relating, which is mainly from the neck up. Feelings partners, aware that feelings have second class status, begin to question the validity of their emotions. Many Thinking tasks in the marriage need attention: money, children, daily logistics, planning, proving who was right in any given situation, and so forth. Feelings are allowed during sex and certain special moments, but they get swamped under by the thinking aspects, and become spaced farther and farther apart.

Year by year, in tiny increments, the Thinking partners become *even more mental* and head-oriented, which is to say increasingly distanced from their inner self and from their feelings. These types don't head down this ever-narrower road with conscious or deliberate intent. In fact, in their preoccupation with events in the outer world, they are not even particularly aware of how they are becoming less and less available emotionally. They feel the pressure of demands on their time but, being in their heads most of the time, they override the limits of their body, telling themselves they are doing it for the betterment of their family and those they care for.

Feelings partners meanwhile also have a tendency to distance from their feelings over that same period of time but for them it is a much more painful experience. Intuitively they know more feeling would add to the potential for wholeness in the relationship and the ultimate betterment of all concerned, but they can only watch as the relationship becomes more and more cerebral and less and less passionate. Instead of being seen by their partner as an ally in a mutually beneficial endeavor, their cries for more feelings in the marriage might be taken as personal attacks or they might be ignored or discounted.

The Onset of Crisis

In the early years of a marriage, Feelings partners go through a predictable sequence of events, though in no particular order. They attempt to accept being ignored in terms of feelings and feeling-values. Sometimes they are on their best behavior, trying to do it all "right." They alternately feel resigned, angry, disappointed, depressed, bored, disgusted, lonely, and so forth—the natural feeling-responses of the Feelings person. In more extreme cases, they may become addicted, overuse medications, and become involved in other self-destructive acts; but mostly they feel an insidious, ever-increasing numbness and despair, a sense that "there must be more to life in marriage than this."

Thinking partners, who are not particularly attuned to their own inner self or to their partner's, tend to be oblivious to interpersonal troubles. Much more capable of detaching themselves, they prefer instead to hold a more *uplifted* view of things (how they "think" things "should" be). They don't see not having feelings as a problem. After a period of time (usually years), as the passion drains out of their marriage, Feelings partners become more and more desperate, and cry out in one form or another. Frequently, they have difficulty putting words on their pain and feel frustrated about that. They don't want to be "fixed," but they do need to be heard and acknowledged—why can't their partner just recognize their *feeling?* But over on the other side, Thinking partners carry on, very busy *doing* things, often nurturing a bit of an inner fantasy about their interpersonal impact, not aware of how numb they, themselves, have become.

Then Feelers get *angry.* Why does that happen? Cerebral partners want passion, but their own feelings have usually been pushed under, which means passion is not readily available to them. That means, in turn, that they *need* the Feeler when they want feelings in their lives, when it's time for feelings to be generated—from *somewhere.* The Feelings partner is *expected* to be the generator of feelings; but, like a stage performer who is getting no energy from the audience, the generator often feels his or her responsibility to be a harrowing (and maddening) experience. Feelers have to carry almost *everything* in the feeling realm. After years of it, the responsibility becomes very, very tiring. In addition, the almost certain promise of being judged and disapproved of for any feeling *not* deemed acceptable adds mightily to the pressure.

If they don't go entirely blank emotionally, Thinking partners have a tendency to set their own feeling temperature according to the feelings their Feelings partner is presenting at any given moment. For example, if their partner is happy, they are happy. If their partner is sad, they are sad. For the Feelings partner, it is like having some very unoriginal, inexpressive person around all the time, mimicking their every movement. And it gets worse.

If the Thinking partners need the Feelings partners to be "happy," so they, themselves, can be happy, even more difficulties emerge. The Thinking partner is going to be invested in

"fixing" or "helping" the Feelers at all times. To be on the receiving end of needing to be "fixed" is not a very welcome experience. Also, when things are emotionally difficult in the
relationship, the Feelings partner always gets identified by the
Thinker as the problem.

All this is very troubling for the Feelings partner, and no
wonder. It is a heavy burden to carry. In exchange for the feelings you put out, you don't get anything vital back (beyond
thoughts). You can't relax because your partner always has an
investment in your being "happy" so he or she can be happy.
In the earlier stages of a marriage, Feelings partners experience
a lot of anger about all this, but eventually, they just begin to
wear down. And the Thinking partners don't "understand"
why. Then the crisis hits—and sadly, a crisis seems required to
get the Thinking partner's full attention.

What happens is simply that the Feelings partners finally
reach the end of their rope. The numbness that has been evolving in the relationship, while either unproblematic or even un-
noticed by their Thinking partners, is no small matter to the
Feelings type. This sense of dulled feeling represents a compromise of values they regard as essential to life itself. Finally,
they come to the awareness, perhaps to their surprise, that they
are on the way out. And this involves more than being on the
way out of the marriage, for the experience to them is like
death looming. They might as well be, they *feel*, on their way
out of life as well. The choice has a felt urgency and, in their
experience, the choice is to act now to restore some life to the
marriage . . . or die.

One day, something snaps and Feelings partners say, "Wait a
minute! All this time together I've been doing my bit to develop
my mental side, and many times felt less-than around a partner who appears more developed in this area. I've fought,
struggled, and put forward my best effort, and my partner has
hardly made a single effort to learn about my side of things,
my strengths. Our relationship is going numb with all these
thoughts and philosophies. It's time for some feelings." They
say, "I demand that you learn about my side of things, about
feelings, yours and mine. And, by the way, it will be great for

both of us if you do so. It will restore some aliveness and juice, which I am in desperate need of. If you don't, I'm afraid this marriage might be over." The Thinking partner is often non-plused by all this, sometimes in shock. It all seems to have appeared so suddenly, out of nowhere.

What Can Marriage Partners Do about All This?

Finally, we come to the question that all Thinking partners like to ask (and the answer they don't like to hear!) *What's to be done about these problems?* Anyone who has been through a marriage will recognize parts of the drama we have laid out here, and they always hope for an easy fix. For some reason, when the big challenges of intimate relating are in front of us, we often tend to live in a bit of a fiction, assuming that the part of inner development involved in learning about feelings is something that ought to just happen by itself, and easily. That is simply not what happens! Acquiring feelings awareness—especially if you were raised in an unemotional family or one that took emotions to extremes, as with alcoholics or other addicts—requires concentrated effort and hard work.

Like important growth in any major area of life, emotional learning requires uncomfortable levels of vulnerability and willingness to move away from places of safety. As therapists, we sigh every time we see people looking for the easy fixes, the Seven Basic No-Risk Overnight Steps that will forever after lead to getting the love you want. People should know that if the road to fulfilling intimacy were a totally safe, happy journey, struggle-free and lacking challenge, a lot more people would have found their way to it.

Please do not interpret this material in terms of rights and wrongs or good and bad, such as, Feelings are superior to Thinking, or vice versa. It is simply a matter of balance. When Thinking partners refuse to find and develop their own Feel-ings self they are out of balance, and the relationship gets out of balance. The road to growth and discovery is blocked. It's like a two-person relay race in which one runner doesn't know how to pick up the baton—the whole race stops there. It's nobody's "fault." Clearly, one runner needs to pick up the baton before both individuals can get to the next layer of discovery.

In your second marriage, get started early with some basic feelings study. It isn't so difficult once the intent is firmly set. We've seen it many times. When the realization finally lands that *both* partners have a lot to learn about feelings and they decide to work on it together instead of fighting about them, big gains are possible for both. She stands a chance of getting the emotional nourishment she has been craving, and he gets more passion and aliveness than he had when he pushed off feelings. The next chapter is for partners who are ready to begin this training.

4

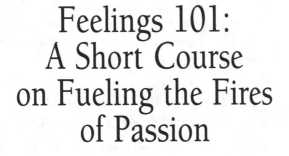

Feelings 101:
A Short Course
on Fueling the Fires
of Passion

Feelings give a marriage energy and passion and keep it alive, vibrant, vulnerable, and truthful. Yet getting partners to learn how to communicate their feelings is one of the biggest challenges of couples' work. Doing so is *very important,* because without feelings from both partners, a relationship always gravitates toward dull and dry. Dull and dry ever so gradually gravitates toward divorce.

For Thinkers especially, learning feelings skills is comparable to learning a new language. You may pick up a few useful phrases without a lot of effort, but in order to have meaningful conversations, you must become a serious student. As a serious student you first acknowledge yourself as a beginner, struggle with basic vocabulary, learn a few rules, study language structures, start saying simple things, practice with native speakers, be prepared to sound stupid, practice a lot more, and fortify your resolve to stay with it (many times over). Then, just when you believe you are finally getting somewhere in the language, you become aware of some frustrating exceptions to the rules and have to take into account the subtle nuances you missed before. But once you get over the initial hurdles, it's worth it. When speaking the new language finally begins to be comfortable, you find yourself in a brand-new land with whole ranges of new possibilities. Learning comes with much less effort—it might even become fun!

The Three Key Elements of Feelings Communication: Locate, Express, Receive

All too often, we see couples who expect to learn more about feelings in a few short days, and they give up when they don't immediately become fluent. *You can't expect to pick up feelings skills overnight.* We'll start here with a few of the basics.* Developing skill in working with feelings in a marriage involves three components: locating the feelings, learning how to express feelings cleanly, and learning how to receive feelings.

Locating Feelings

Before we can do anything with feelings, we need to be able to find them—and that is more challenging than most Thinking types want to believe. During a week-long group training, we may ask individuals and couples what they are feeling twenty-five, or more, times a day. In the beginning, the individuals must really struggle to come up with a *feeling word* that honestly reflects what's going on within them at the moment, and it takes determined effort to stay with it. The first response is often a thinking response: "I don't know." But when they are pressed to explore further, they slowly begin uncovering their feelings.

*If you are predominately a Feelings type, this may seem too familiar to you. Nonetheless we suggest you stay alert because, under pressure, in intimacy, Feelings types are often not as skilled with feelings as they believe they are. If you are a Thinking type, please read on without judgement and give feelings a chance. Both types have to realize that book-learning a language can only take you so far, serious students will do best to engage a teacher.

The ability to become aware of and identify our own feelings at any given moment ought to be automatic, but most of us haven't opened clear pathways from our feeling experience to our present state of awareness. Instead, we—men and women alike—often hold the feelings down or filter them through our mind, and their immediacy is lost to us. We tend to run on automatic pilot, unaware of our feelings.

Shifting out of automatic takes constant effort, and locating feelings is an art that takes practice. We must be willing to suspend our belief that thought rules everything, and to interrupt the habitual way we relate to our intimates. Ready? Let's begin.

Step One: What Am I Feeling? In order to begin to locate your feelings, you need to ask yourself the following question as often as possible each day: "What am I feeling right now?" Don't settle for the answer "Nothing," or "I don't know," or "Fine," or "Good," or "Bad." These are mental evaluations, not feelings. It sounds simple, but our experience indicates that fewer than one in a hundred people will actually follow through with this exercise for more than a week. The serious student of intimate relating clearly has to make a better effort. To reach through to your feelings means attuning to the more subtle realms of your inner nature. And when you finally do identify the true feeling, you will experience the sense that truth has been uncovered.

Ask yourself now, "What am I feeling?" Search in your body. Allow yourself to be a little more vulnerable than usual. Go a little deeper. Slow down; take some time—feelings are hard to reach when you are rushing.

Step Two: Practicing Feelings To deepen your intimate relationship, set aside some time each day to practice finding feelings with your intimate partner. From time to time, ask your partner what he or she is feeling (and be willing to share your own feelings, too). Have some fun with it. Let go of judgments. Allow yourself a beginner's mind. Practice when the relationship is running smoothly. Do it before the bigger feelings are spilling out. If the relationship has been emotionally stuffed for a long time, know that you have to apply the type of energy required to turn a battleship, slow and steady.

Remember that allowing a feeling has nothing to do with *doing* anything about it. One of the reasons Thinking types are afraid of feelings is that they believe once they open to a feeling, they will need to "do" something about it. A feeling is a feeling and can't harm anybody. It's the need to *do something* that creates the problems.

Expressing Feelings

We frequently encounter individuals who say they know what their feelings are but don't express them. In an intimate relationship, when partners "know" their feelings but are not able to articulate them, it is not that much different from not being able to locate them at all. It's like holding a secret. That person may know but nobody else does. In order to deepen intimacy, partners have to be able to locate what is happening on the inside *and* be able to communicate it.

Generally speaking, there are "positive" feelings (like happiness, joy, excitement) and the more "difficult" feelings (like pain, sadness, and anger). It is unfortunate that many partners even have difficulty expressing their positive feelings to their intimates, but that is usually more a matter of developing the resolve to become a little bolder. Challenging as that can be, we are more interested in those feelings that are more difficult to express.

Expressing Difficult Feelings A feeling not expressed is a feeling held back. Contrary to what our rational self might tell us, holding back a feeling does *not* eliminate its presence or its effect. In fact, we discover that a held-back feeling ultimately intensifies. Let's take resentment as an example.

You have before you a couple, and both partners are filled with resentment. They want to pretend otherwise because they want to be "nice." But you can see right away that they are distanced from each other emotionally. This couple also has a lot of positive feelings for each other, but they avoid sharing their resentments—and, ironically, the resentments are what show. Afraid of acknowledging and expressing their resentments, both partners have pushed them away, perhaps for months and years. Rather than producing the desired effect of creating happiness and joy, this rejection or denial of feeling-truth has resulted in a large underground pool of resentments that is spilling over into their lives.

Now any reasonably skilled helper could assist this couple to bypass the resentments a little longer and focus on heightening so-called positive feelings in each partner. The rational theory about this might be: Continue to heighten the positive aspects, the pressure will be alleviated, and everything will turn around. According to this model, *all difficult feelings can be bargained or rationalized away*. Effect the correct strategy, incorporate the appropriate insight, and you find your way to "happy" (and stay there happily ever after). That's the way the head looks at feeling.

In a younger relationship, the partners might follow through on the so-called positive track with each other and ignore their resentments for some time. But the partners we are talking about have been around a little longer. Pretending this large pool of accumulated resentments is not in the middle of their marriage just won't work. Partners who are sitting on resentments simply don't follow through with assignments to be positive. They easily go sour on each other, withhold from each other, or become defensive at the slightest provocation. Bickering breaks out too frequently. In other words, the underlying resentments just keep popping back through in one form or another when the determination to remain uplifted fades even slightly.

Now take the same couple and help them get started expressing their resentments to each other. Neither wants to do it. It's difficult and unpleasant, perhaps even painful. Partners somehow think they have been fooling each other, and they are afraid to have things out in the open. But they each finally agree to give it a try, which means expressing their own feelings and agreeing to listen to the other person's resentful feelings.

Both begin hesitantly. They have no training for clean expression of their more difficult feelings. Everyone takes a deep breath. We help them to set some ground rules. One begins, the other only listens. We ask each what their feelings are, as resentments are voiced, nothing more. Then the other expresses resentments, carrying on until he or she is heard. Some reflect clear-cut injustices. Some are picayune. Some go back years. There are few real surprises, because the other already had a sense about the existence of the grievances. Once in a while, though, something brand-new and revelatory comes through.

Before long, the relief is palpable. The air starts to clear. Partners begin to look each other in the eye again. Some of the disclosures were difficult to hear; much more was not so hard to hear. Even the painful ones are better than frozen silences or the passive-aggressive stuff that has been coming. Now other feelings come up. More communication occurs. There are a few defenses, many more clarifications, and a couple of apologies. More relief. More willingness to communicate. More feelings. There is no need to work at heightening positive feelings, they just start happening. We can't count the number of times we have seen this happen.

We're not trying to make this sound easy, because it isn't. A couple in real trouble probably shouldn't attempt to do this without some professional help, because it won't work if partners are hyper-reactive to each other. But we know that when the process is undertaken with sincere intent to clear the feelings, it can be very helpful at opening up blocked relationships.

Holding back so-called negative feelings eventually results in a holding back of so-called positive feelings. Trying to live just in positive feelings only necessitates putting on a mask. Living behind a mask sooner or later leads to a phoniness. Phoniness leads to a type of numbness. On the other hand, open up the feelings and you get positive ones *and* you get negative ones, but *life* and *passion* follow. In short, the option is this: Deal with all of your feelings or go numb!

We would ask that the student of feelings consider one more point about expressing. *Holding a feeling back takes energy.* A withheld feeling that is getting more intense takes ever-increasing amounts of energy to hold it back. Energy used to hold back feelings is not available for living life. Before long, the withholder of feelings experiences an energy drain. If the withholding carries on long enough, that person ends up with low-grade depression, maybe followed by deeper or longer-lasting depressions and no passion for life. The rule is this: Too much holding back in an intimate relationship will kill it.

Now, expressing a feeling has to do with moving feeling energy within an *individual*. It adds to the circulation of an individual's emotional energy (the flow of which keeps the heart from getting clogged). This is the flow of life itself. This movement of energy can be a cathartic process for the individual and lead to relief, but how does this all work in an intimate relationship? Bottom line, the expression of a feeling doesn't lead to much sustained gain in an intimate relationship unless it is received. And this is a *very* important part of the training.

Receiving Feelings

Learning to *locate* feelings involves developing greater self-awareness. Learning to *express* feelings requires becoming vulnerable and learning how to move the energy of feelings from inside ourselves into the world. *Receiving* a feeling completes the circuit of energy-sharing in a relationship and ensures emotional nourishment in intimacy.

Take a simple example. Janice expresses affection in a clear, clean way to her partner, Bill. He turns his back, changes the topic, attempts to discuss the meaning of love, withdraws into a shell, judges, tries to talk her out of her feeling, attempts to teach something, or is off somewhere in thought or diverted attention. *None of these low-risk responses shows any indication that he received the expressed feeling.* It's a very mixed experience for Janice. As an individual, she has some relief about expressing her feeling. It was a leap in vulnerability, a risk that took some courage. She moved forward as a human being. But as a partner in a marriage, she *experiences a hollowness because her feeling was obviously not received.*

If nonreceiving is the norm in her marriage, it is clear where things are heading. She brought forward a part of her inner experience, a part of who she was, and it was not received. When her feeling isn't received, she is going to feel rejected, pained, hurt, discounted, probably angry. A few rejections like this and she is going to be much more cautious about bringing herself forward again in a feeling way. The journey toward numbness and stagnation has begun.

Now we look at the same expression of feeling, but this time it is received. Bill, upon hearing about her feeling, takes a second or two before responding. He searches inside himself for the feeling in him that arose in response to the feeling she just expressed. Once he has located that feeling, he says he is warm, excited, fearful, happy, sad, sexual, or whatever (it could practically be any feeling). The fact that he gives her back a feeling response from inside himself gives her an indication he was affected in *some* way by her expression. In other words, her expressed feeling landed within him and generated something palpable. The evidence of this was his expression, in return, of his own feeling.

Janice might have been hoping for a particular response, perhaps even a different response than she got; but just knowing that her feeling landed inside him (was received) helps her to feel more involved and interested. Whatever feeling came back from him is likely to have generated another feeling inside of her, which she can now express back to him. As this happens, there is the possibility in this relationship of further energy and development. No one knows where it will go next, *but it is moving* and the partners are involved, getting to know more about each other, and probably enhancing their intimacy.

What most beginners don't realize is that *all* feelings need to be received—even the more difficult ones, like anger. We'll study that idea more thoroughly in chapter 5, but first we need to better understand this idea of receiving feelings. As we said, feelings need to be received to complete the circuit of passion. When a feeling is received, receivers of the feeling are more energized by the feeling that was expressed. The expressers feel more relaxed and calm and ultimately loving when their feelings have been received by the other. Both partners end up more emotionally satisfied.

How do we know when a feeling has been received? How do we know when sharing our inner world has made an impact on our partner? We know when the partner shows some kind of response. One way to know that a feeling has been received is when it generates a feeling in the other person *and is expressed back.*

When a feeling is expressed, and it lands on the partner, and the partner locates the feeling that emerges in response and shares that feeling, *energy flows in the relationship*—far more energy than any rational, analytical exchange could have provided. Here we have two inner selves sharing actual energy with each other. Both partners experience nourishment as a result of the exchange. Defenses are down. New awarenesses are possible. Movement is possible. Intimacy is enhanced.

Emotional Tennis

We all understand the basics of an enriching philosophical exchange. One partner generates an idea and expresses it. If the conversation is to continue in a balanced and enriching way, the receiver takes in the message, works it over mentally and sends it back. The original expresser receives that message, digests it, and sends it back again. This we all do all the time— from our minds.

A feeling exchange works the same way. Here's an image that might help: We call it "Emotional Tennis."

To keep feelings communication alive in a relationship, we need two partners, each committed to check inside before responding, each on his or her own court, ready to play. One serves a feeling to the other. If the partner to whom the serve comes refuses to receive the feeling, or misses it completely, the game can't progress. If the receiver keeps shouting that he or she can't play this game and refuses to make any effort to learn, the game cannot progress. If one partner insists on playing another kind of game—say, the game of "Intellectual Tennis"—and wants, in response to the feeling serve, to return with a rational discourse, because that is what he or she is good at, it's an invitation to a power struggle. Sooner or later the server, who wants to play Emotional Tennis, is going to get angry. Nobody is home over on the other side; nobody's there to play. Eventually, if the nonreceiver continues in this way, the server is simply going to give up, pack his or her feelings up, and look around for someone who *will* play.

Now, suppose the receiver (we'll say "he," but it could just as easily be "she") steps up to address the feeling that just got served. He has to make an effort to catch that feeling. He has to be alert and reach for it. As he takes it in, he has to allow it into his body. Just as his mind would turn over an idea in Intellectual Tennis, and look at it from all sides, his body needs some time to explore around the feeling that was served. It generally takes longer to process a feeling than an idea, but eventually a feeling will emerge—*and then he has to send it back across the net.* Receiving it is hugely different from just watching it go by or fending it off. It's a skill, one that can be learned. But the plain fact is that in order to keep the game going, *something* has to be done on his side in response to the serve *and* something has to be sent back across. When this happens, energy is exchanged and the game builds speed and excitement.

Then the original server (let's say "she") must be alert for that returned feeling, field it with her body, and send it back across in a like manner. (Chances are she thinks she is better at this than she really is, so she has to stay alert, too.) As soon as someone starts serving back rationalizations—excuses, reasons for this and that, explanations in the place of playing—the game is finished, because there is no game if both players aren't playing the same game. It is tough to keep up this game because it requires significant levels of vulnerability on each side, whereas exchanging intellectualizations requires almost none.

At this point, the Thinking partner might want to ask why there need to be *two* games in a relationship. Can't everything be accomplished with intellectual tennis? No, it can't. There are two types of partners, and each partner needs to get a bit of the game that is most satisfying to that person. Really, that is reason enough for partners who want to sustain a balanced, mutually rewarding relationship. But there is more to it than that—let's talk about a few aspects of feeling communication that we have only alluded to so far.

Feelings: A Straight Line to the Truth

The Thinking type person has a hard time believing that in intimacy feeling is a faster avenue to the truth than intellectualization—until, usually in a therapeutic setting, they are restricted to expressing themselves only from what they are feeling. In our work with couples, we learned a long time ago that the most complicated, convoluted, circular relationship issues can be worked out in relatively short order if both partners are confined to expressing their feelings to each other. When both partners' essential truth is out in the open, we see huge leaps in awareness. And awareness leads to the resolution of problems.

Consider this: Do lie detectors measure words? No. They measure events in the body. Anyone who watches television knows that the clever manipulation of words is used all the time to create convenient realities. The body, however, can't lie. The message that comes along with a feeling arrives directly from the inner being and exposes who we are. We can easily organize words to fool ourselves; but our feelings, which come to us from our inner nature, tell the truth.

Let's look at a few examples of Thinking statements *versus* the Feeling expression of the same experience. Notice how the Feeling statement presents a much more direct and vulnerable assessment of present truth:

- "You're a controller" (Thinking) *versus* "I'm feeling powerless around you" (Feeling).
- "The way you spend money is going to bankrupt us" (Thinking) *versus* "I feel fearful about our financial future" or "I'm feeling used" or "I'm feeling angry" (Feeling)

- "You're acting so sad these days; why don't you just get over it?" (Thinking) *versus* "When you are down, I feel hopeless" (Feeling).
- "You come to bed on a night when we both know we're going to make love and you're all uptight, it makes me want to kick you out" (Thinking) *versus* "I feel hurt and angry when I am given such a low place on your list of priorities" (Feeling).
- "You're always hugging our child; what about me?" (Thinking) *versus* "I feel alone and neglected. I'm feeling hungry for your touch" (Feeling).
- "You are so mean to our child" (Thinking) *versus* "I felt angry when you yelled at our child" (Feeling).
- "Are you hungry now?" (Thinking) *versus* "I feel hungry" (Feeling).
- "Why don't you pick up your clothes?" (Thinking) *versus* "I feel scattered and confused when our bedroom is in such chaos" (Feeling).
- "You are such a flirt" (Thinking) *versus* "I feel angry when you look at other men" (Feeling).
- "I think we're having a power struggle here" (Thinking) *versus* "I'm feeling fearful or angry or whatever . . ." (Feeling).

Both statements are addressing essentially the same issue, but the second gets to the truth of what is really happening inside the speaker. The information in the first statements typically offers an insight about the *other's* shortcomings, typically putting the partner on the defensive and inviting a like response. The second statement presents a vulnerable assessment of the speaker's own inner state; it is much more revealing, more truthful, much less safe. The feeling statement adds new information and doesn't tend to drive the listening partner into defense. Thus, it has a much better chance of being heard, raising awareness, and leading someplace other than to an argument. Only by getting personal is there a chance of getting anywhere real and lasting on the issues that are being raised. (Of course both partners have to be willing to play this game:

If one continually lets down defenses and other continues to respond intellectually, nothing can be gained.)

Getting Started

How do two people who are in large part blind to their feelings and who have spent a lifetime covering them over suddenly start communicating on this level? We will list a few steps that can help partners in relationship get started. Determined individuals can make a lot of progress if they are willing to follow these steps. Nevertheless, as we've said before (and this is not just a commercial for therapists), training oneself to become more aware on the emotional level is easier to learn with assistance. Why? Because we are all subject to our own delusions about ourselves. Since few of us received adequate modeling and training at the earlier stages of life, longstanding habits get in the way. Also, at first, partners who are stalemated have difficulty listening to and thus receiving this help from each other. Awareness of feelings is new, unfamiliar territory, and partners need to find someone whose guidance and input they value.

With that caveat, here are seven suggestions you can use to begin to enhance your feeling skills:

1. Set an intent to learn all you can about feelings—and resolve to stick with it.
2. Ask yourself regularly if you are in your head or your body, thinking or feeling. If you can become aware of your body, you are more present. If you are only in your head, figuring things out, the chances are you are in defense and (unconsciously) looking for a way to get control. If you are in your head, see if you can relocate into your body. What is going on inside your body? What are you feeling? *Take the time* to go inward and find out. Allow yourself some room for imperfection; this is a new skill you are trying to develop.
3. Focus on using "I feel" statements, especially when you become aware that a circular argument has started. Make sure the word that follows "feel" actually is a feeling before you allow yourself any words to elaborate.

4. Be alert. If you come out with something like "I feel *that* . . ." or "I feel *you* . . . ," stop. You are not feeling, nor are any of the words that follow likely to have anything to do with feelings. You are in your head. Go back and see if you can come forth with "I feel . . ." and have it actually be a feeling. If you bypass this step, you will get nowhere.

5. Ask your partner (if he or she is willing to join you in this exploration) for his or her feelings. Observe whether your partner is expressing a feeling or an intellectualization. Observe your own inner response to the announced feelings, not your analysis of the other's feelings.

6. Have patience. You and your partner may not be able to locate the precise feelings until sometime after the fact, but if you have the perseverance to keep on working with this approach, the delay time will shorten.

7. If you recognize what you were feeling sometime after the fact, try to articulate it even though the moment has passed. This will help you anchor the awareness and shorten the reaction time in the future.

Practice Giving and Receiving Feelings

Get together with your partner and commit to spend ten minutes each, each day, talking to your partner using only feeling words. That means sitting down face-to-face, simply tracking the feelings that are going on inside. Say, "I'm feeling. . . . [followed by naming the feeling]" and then allow some elaboration, but not too much, before allowing another feeling. You'll quickly discover this is a lot more challenging than you might think, and ten minutes can be a long time. Notice the tendency to say nothing instead. Notice how much more effort is required to dig deeper. Over time, you will notice more truth coming out and also how much more vulnerability is required to keep up this type of dialogue.

The receiving partner should say *nothing* during the ten minutes. The temptation to coach, teach, ask questions (which always takes expressers more to their intellect) is just too great, especially at the beginning. Just listen, practice taking in the other's feelings, and when the time is up, first talk about the feelings generated as a result of the other's expression. Notice your level of connection as a result of this ten minutes, as compared to what it might be after a philosophical exchange.

A Final Note:
The Effects of Smoking on Feelings

What do people get out of smoking? Sometimes people smoke to stimulate themselves, in particular their mental processes; sometimes they smoke to calm themselves. Which way is it then: Are cigarettes a stimulant or a depressant?

The way we see it, cigarettes are *feeling inhibitors*. Feel powerless deep down? Smoke a cigarette, cut that feeling, and be more ready to go out and face the world (stimulant). Feel angry? Smoke a cigarette, sever that feeling, and it's easier to cope (calming effect). Feel fearful? The feeling goes up in smoke. And on it goes.

But what happens when you stop smoking? All the feelings that you have pushed down over the years come welling up, particularly the uncomfortable ones. Better to grab a cigarette and push them down again. If people want to interfere with their life-force in this way, that is totally up to them. But there is an element of counterproductivity involved in trying to get more in touch with feelings and become more alive while continuing to smoke. It's one foot on the gas with the other foot on the brake. We believe a similar process occurs with many other addictive substances, but drawing conclusions about them would be out of our realm of experience. For now, we simply say this: If you smoke and you want to begin learning about feelings, quit smoking and see what happens.

5

The Positive Power
of Anger in an Intimate
Relationship

Anyone can become angry—that is easy. But to be angry with the
right person, to the right degree, at the right time, for the right
purpose, and in the right way—that is not easy.

ARISTOTLE, *The Nicomachean Ethics*

More than two thousand years have passed since Aristotle
wrote the words that begin this chapter, and all kinds of material has been written by all kinds of people on this most
challenging and most human of emotions. Sadly, in our view
anyway, a lot of that material has the core message that the
best way to deal with anger is by not dealing with it. Anger is
held as an unenlightened, potentially dangerous part of the
human condition that ought to be transcended, rationalized
away, overpowered by will, diluted by sweet thoughts, or by-
passed in some other way. We hold a different viewpoint.

A world without anger might be a child's ideal, but in real
life it doesn't work that way—particularly for those of us who
commit to long-term intimacies. Soon enough, partners in all
intimate relationships realize that fewer situations in life are

better designed to get under our skin (and bring everything out!). No two people can live for long periods in close proximity without conflict in regard to wants. Boundaries get violated. A partner will be thoughtlessly selfish or act unjustly from time to time. All these things lead to frustration, and frustration is just the tip of anger.

When it comes to dealing with anger, we have two choices. First, we can push it away by ignoring, repressing, or denying it. This strategy makes life a little simpler, but there is a cost. After a period of withholding feelings of anger, other powerful feelings drain out of the relationship as well, most noticeably sexual ones. There are other costs, too. Anger that has been suppressed for a long time has a way of seeping out in sneaky, passive ways (such as via judgmentalism, snide jabs, supercilious attitudes, edgy humor, overspending, withholding that which is most desired by the other) or blowing out at unexpected points in ways that can be destructive. Our other option is to bite the bullet and decide to develop some skills to deal with our anger.

Having witnessed the outcomes of both of these choices, we've come to the conclusion that developing anger skills is an important relationship task. Genuine intimacy requires two whole humans bringing all of who they are (or as much as they are able) to the relationship. Feelings of anger—part of the experience of aliveness and passion—are part of what being human is all about. Hiding from anger means hiding part of oneself, and this means presenting a mask to the world and not really being fully present in the truth of who we are. How can partners who are hiding from part of themselves expect to have an abiding, authentic intimacy with each other?

Developing anger skills comes much more easily from direct experience than from the written word, but difficulties in this realm come up so often in our work with couples that we believe it is important to include something on the topic. It is not that couples aren't capable of firing off loud words at each other. Everyone can do that! What they can't do is be with the powerful energies of anger and angry feelings, in a direct and constructive way. Our intent in this chapter is to present a few basic ideas to inspire you, if you are lacking in this area, to get a start on acquiring some skills. If you want to explore the topic a little more, see our book *Dancing in the Dark*.

Before we start let's make another thing perfectly clear. The material in this chapter is geared toward intimate partners who have made a long-term commitment to be together and to work out all the differences, conflicts, and complex feelings that will inevitably arise between them. We are not talking about anger in the workplace, or anger between strangers or even casual friends. We are not talking about anger toward children. We are not talking about people who hide from their inadequacies by attempting to gain power (consciously or unconsciously) over others through misuse of anger energy. We also have no intention of addressing partners who are perfectly happy pushing anger out of their relationship, if that is what works for them.

Roger and Valerie: Anger Basics

Let's get a few of the anger basics by looking in on Roger and Valerie. Now in their late thirties, they've been married five years. It's a second marriage for Valerie, who was married to her first partner for ten years. This is the first marriage for Roger. Clearly, there is a lot of affection between these two, but the loving passion between them has been fading. In fact, lately it seems like Valerie has been alternating between angry and depressed and Roger doesn't understand what her problem is. If we were to summarize the lines they spoke in our office it would go something like this:

SHE: I feel so angry and he says he doesn't feel anger. I know he has a lot of anger, and when he says he doesn't, it makes me feel like I'm crazy.

HE: I can't figure out why she is so angry. I only get angry when I have a good reason. Why can't we just work things out in a sensible, rational way so ongoing peace would be possible?

SHE: See what I mean? He totally denies his anger. And not only that, he won't let me have mine. He just runs away whenever I get angry.

HE: Sure, I leave when she gets as angry as she has been recently. It doesn't feel safe to me and I don't need it.

SHE: I want a man who can match me in my feelings.

HE: If I'm expected to be angry all the time, like her, I'm not sure I'm in the right relationship.

We've heard variations of these lines in many marriages. Let's take the time now to break things down and look at what is going on.

Express and Receive Anger

For the moment let's set aside the issue of whether Roger has anger or not and deal with what we know for sure. Valerie is angry and has been for some time. Telling her to get rid of it is not going to help. Roger not dealing with her anger and hiding from it is not going to help. In order to move through to more successful relating, two things have to happen. One, Valerie has to learn how to express her anger in a way that is clean, clear, and capable of being received. Two, Roger has to recognize that Valerie has anger that can't be denied; and, by not receiving her, he is actually contributing to the problem he is facing.

What is a clean expression of anger? Let's go with Valerie first. Here's the situation she faces. Living a passionate life is important to her. Instinctively, she knows that living a passionate life means being able to access the complete range of her feelings. She knows she has anger; but it's a powerful feeling, and she's not much more comfortable with it than Roger is. Like most people who have no training with anger expression, her tendency is to swallow it. She has done this for a couple of years in her marriage with Roger, but she can't take it any more.

Now her anger is pushing through, despite her efforts to control it.

She doesn't want to scare Roger, nor does she want to lose him. She just knows where all this went in her first marriage and she doesn't want to repeat it again. In her first marriage, she gave herself away by being a good girl. Like many individuals who deny their anger, she redirected it against herself and went through protracted periods of low-grade depression without really understanding why. By now she senses that is not a healthy thing to do, for her physical body as well as her emotional one. Not only had she resolved not to let that same process repeat in her second marriage, she was getting older and had more of a desire to be in her woman. Good girls might be able to live their lives without expressing anger, but a mature woman can't.

Not knowing how to use her anger energy, and having years of anger stuffed up inside her, she makes a common mistake. She either expresses her anger by being cold and withdrawn, or she lets fly with a lot of high-decibel words—typically words that find fault with her partner or support a self-righteous position relative to him. In the first instance, she makes her partner aware she is angry but does nothing to move her anger energy—it's an adult sulk. In the second instance, the so-called expression of anger is truly more about punishing and gaining power than moving her anger energy. We know this because her words are filled with "you" statements and her attention is primarily directed toward proving her point, or proving she is "right" or proving he has "wronged" her. As we shall discover, expressing anger (by our definition, at least) and belittling another are two different things.

Anger Expression: Ground Rules

At this first level of anger training, we establish some commonsense ground rules about honoring each other's physical boundaries and then we take away the words when partners are expressing anger to each other. We keep it that way until partners become much more conscious with their anger expressions. It is much too easy to get carried away with thoughtless words that only engender defensive responses (which usually ends up going nowhere).

Imagine yourself, right now, expressing anger to your partner in this way: You are not allowed to threaten his or her physical space. You are not allowed to use words. Your mission is to send anger energy from your belly as you maintain eye contact with your partner a few feet away from you. You are encouraged to use sounds. If you want to pound pillows, that's okay.

Reading about it makes it sound simple; but if you allowed yourself to actually try this, you might discover that expressing anger energy, contrary to our usual belief about anger, actually requires vulnerability (a vulnerability most of us avoid by opting to sulk silently or hiding behind a stream of words).

In the early stages of training with anger, we ask individuals to practice expressing anger in this way in order to help them better understand the nature of anger. Most people equate anger with potential for abuse. In truth, anger is anger and abuse is abuse. Expressing anger is a movement of a feeling energy—it has nothing to do with hurting anybody or doing anything to anybody. Abuse is about misuse of power, with an intention to cause harm. Because abuse can come with anger attached, many individuals have come to invariably link the two. Following that line of reasoning, if you want to eliminate abuse you have to eliminate anger. That is faulty thinking. In fact, we have found that people who refuse to express their anger in a healthy way (move their anger energy as it comes up for them) are those who are most likely to abuse.

In our opinion, learning to express anger constructively is a good skill for everyone to acquire—not just for emotional health but physical health as well. We highly recommend it. But for partners in intimate relationships it is particularly important. In fact anger, used appropriately, can serve a productive purpose in intimacy. But in order for that to happen, partners have to learn how to receive anger.

Anger Needs to Be Received

Here's the situation Roger faces. As a child, Roger found anger too powerful an energy to handle. So, as a young person operating naturally within an either/or modality, he "made" a decision. Anger was "bad" and potentially hurtful. He wanted to be "good" and not hurt anyone. Succeeding at being good meant pushing away anger.

This decision served him for many years. He went ahead with many endeavors in life and succeeded as the nice guy. Then, a little later in life, he married. In the first years his strategy worked, and Valerie cooperated by playing good girl (because she had made a similar decision). Now Roger suddenly finds himself with an angry woman and can't figure out what is going on. What does he need to know?

When a decision is made as a child to handle something in a particular way, and no effort is made to challenge or update that decision, although the body grows chronologically into adulthood, that person is still operating with the original child's decision. Not having been taught anything different and not knowing how to look at himself in any other way, Roger has ended up in a blind spot. If that blind spot was left unchallenged, as it might well have been if he had continued to live as a bachelor for the rest of his life, likely he would have never revisited that child's decision—he would have just carried on with the same strategy to the end of his days. But he decided to marry a woman who can't hide her anger for the rest of her days, and now his old strategy won't work. Some new way of coping is called for.

There is something else Roger doesn't yet realize. As he defends against Valerie's anger by using his intellect to make this seem to be her problem, he is essentially putting up a wall against her anger. There is no place for Valerie's anger to go. In his mind Roger believes that he is protecting himself from something "bad" and therefore doing something "good" for himself, just like he learned to do in his earlier years. The problem is that as he defends against Valerie's anger and refuses to deal with it (or, as we say, refuses to receive it), the anger energy that she expresses essentially gets bounced back to her. As the anger energy bounces back to her, she has two options. She gets even angrier, or she closes off to him. Having witnessed this same phenomenon in many relationships, we know the ultimate outcome. After years of not having her angry feelings received, and getting angrier all the while, eventually she will give up trying to share any of her energy with him. She will either go numb inside the marriage, or go outside the marriage to get her intimacy needs met, or both.

In an earlier chapter, we walked through a case example where one partner refused to receive feelings of affection from the other. If that process were to carry on, the outcome would be very obvious. What most people don't realize is that it works that way with *all* feelings—which, of course, includes anger. Valerie's anger is part of who she is. It is her feeling, and her feeling is a direct reflection of her. As Roger continues to push off Valerie's feelings, he is pushing off Valerie, as a woman. Not only does he end up with an angrier Valerie, he ends up with a partner who feels rejected for the person she is.

Now let's go back to Roger, assuming he is willing to digest any of this information (which might not be possible if he is totally defended and in a serious blind spot about his real emotional age in regard to anger). He might say, "Hah, what am I supposed to be, some sort of garbage dump for her feelings? Am I just supposed to lay down and eat her anger all day long? If I were to do that I would lose my self-respect as a man. It's not worth it. I'd rather take the pain of quitting and go find myself an always friendly and loving, peaceful woman."

Roger has only been married once, so we might forgive him for being a little naive. He hasn't learned yet that *all* women have anger (good-girl or kind-mother types may not show it as readily, but they have it too). His choice is either to learn to be with anger or give up on being with an adult woman. Locked into his earlier strategy, he has never even tried to receive Valerie's anger to find out what might happen.

Receiving Anger Energy

Let's assume that Valerie has learned something about expressing anger. She realizes now it is not about changing Roger, or dominating, or abusing, or avenging, or proving anything. It is really about expressing her feeling for herself. She agrees to make that effort.

Now Roger is freed up from having to automatically defend. In return, he agrees to attempt to receive her anger and not deflect it in some way. But since he has never received her anger before, or even heard of the concept, he doesn't know what that would look like.

We explain to Roger that she is essentially sending the energy of one of her most intense feelings from her body to his. If he is receiving that feeling into his body, he will in turn experience a feeling. If he shares that feeling back with her, that will give an indication that he has received her feeling. To satisfy his skeptical mind, we suggest setting up a little experiment.

Valerie begins expressing her anger (in the nonverbal way described earlier) and keeps on expressing it. Roger goes through all his mental paces to try to cope.

At first he analyzes her: He's not receiving anything.

Another part of him judges her anger: He's not receiving anything.

Then he asks questions about why she is angry: Still not receiving.

Then he suggests she count from ten back to one and breathe: Still not receiving.

Then he becomes aloof and tells her it is *her* anger. It has nothing to do with him, so she ought to get over it: Definitely not receiving!

Then he opens a little and discovers he feels anger. Maybe he is receiving or maybe he is just defending by mobilizing some kind of counter-effort, we don't know yet. In any case, all these responses do nothing to alleviate Valerie's anger.

Valerie has still not exhausted her anger—it's been building up for a long time. She carries on expressing. We encourage

Roger to come down from his mind and enter a little more into his body. Taking in a breath or two on the receiving end of anger always helps! Behind his tendency to defend, what is he feeling?

After a brief search of his feelings, he says he is feeling a little fear. For the first time we know he is beginning to receive her feeling. Her energy is engendering a feeling in him. It doesn't matter one bit which feeling comes up for him, as long as he is honest about whatever he is feeling. As he begins to get more comfortable with anger energy, and his child begins to calm down a bit inside, he realizes he is not being harmed by her feeling energy. Now he feels some excitement as he experiences Valerie expressing her anger at him in a lioness's roar.

As part of this experiment, after each response from Roger, we've been checking back to Valerie to see where her anger is going. We've already learned that all his nonreceiving responses did nothing to change her anger. But as soon as he shows some sign of receiving her anger, she starts to experience a feeling *other* than anger. Feelings like relief, happiness, and strangely enough, love and affection eventually begin to come through for her.

We have been witnessing this same experience for years, and the outcome is always the same. When that first breakthrough occurs and anger gets received for the first time, a stuck couple immediately makes a shift to a more open position. The person who has been fighting off anger is shocked to discover that doing the exact opposite of what they have habitually done for years leads to the effect they had originally been desiring: more openness, more relief, more peace, and more affection.

What About Roger's Anger?

As with any new skill, anger training becomes more complex after the first breakthrough. But to make the shift from anger-as-power or anger-needing-to-do-something to anger-as-movement-of-inner-energy is very significant. To make the shift from defending anger to receiving it is equally important. It may not come across in written word very easily but in direct experience it is a profound experience.

Now we've got to get more serious with Roger. We know that after five years as an ordinary man in a marriage, the last months of which have been spent with a wife who has been doing quite a bit of raging, some time of which she has been closed to him sexually, Roger has been experiencing some bit of anger. After a lifetime of pushing it away, it's not something that comes quickly to him. We also have to remember that anger is definitely not his idea of "fun" and he doesn't particularly want to shift a long-standing habit. We also have to remember that clean expressions of anger actually require vulnerability. (Don't believe it? Try standing up in front of a mirror and making an angry sound right this moment.)

We also know that anger exists in the body all the time, just like all the other feelings. Actors bring them up on demand and we worship them for being able to do so. Being accustomed to living through our minds, however, most of us don't seem to get the idea that we all have all feelings all the time.

Roger slowly acknowledges that he does have anger from time to time, but just not now. "Maybe later," he says. If we let Roger off the hook at this moment, we know that "later" he won't be any more inclined to develop his anger skills than he is at this moment. So we encourage him to bypass all his resistance and try bringing up his anger now. If he has to remember a past injustice and hold that picture in his mind in order to give himself permission to be angry, so be it. (Later in our training we would expect him to do this without needing to conjure up the past.)

We know that Roger is going to struggle at this point because he has been hiding from and intellectualizing away his anger for years. It is going to take some effort to keep him on point until he takes the leap of actually testing his anger out. But we keep prodding him because we know, until he is willing to do that, nothing will shift. Nothing will shift because he will get no real-world evidence that will help him change the belief system he formed as a child. He doesn't realize yet that his refusal to experience his own anger has meant that Valerie has been forced to feel the anger for the two of them.

As he is about to attempt some anger expression, Roger's self-judgment comes in. No silly sounds for him. Doesn't want to look stupid. No pounding of pillows, that's just some therapeutic hokum from the sixties. To bring it up now would just be pretending, and he doesn't want to be phony. He might go out of control and be dangerous. These therapists are cracked. Maybe he'll scare the kids in the neighboring block. . . . If pressed to the point, he'd just prefer to *talk* about his anger, not experience it directly, not express the feeling of it. Roger has reached his Rubicon. He can stay with these thoughts, which are only slightly past his child's decision about anger, or he can take the leap and see what happens.

Let's say we can convince him to try on his scientist's hat once again and try another experiment. We can't find out anything for sure until we are willing to try. Through a mixture of coaxing, cajoling, and coaching we get Roger to try moving some anger energy. This time he takes the leap.

At first, Valerie is in shock. She hasn't seen this kind of energy from the old boy before. His eyes are flashing and a lion's roar is coming at her. Her first instinct is to defend (just like him). We get through that. Then maybe some fear. We get through that. Then she starts to experience some relief. Just getting his anger straight on instead of in the passive, hidden ways is a huge relief. To know that he is capable of more than young-boy-like reactions to his anger is a relief. To know she doesn't have to carry all the anger is a relief. To see that he has emotional energy and some boundaries to go with it is a relief. To know that maybe they can grow together into the more powerful emotions is a relief. Then she begins to experience some excitement, and then affection and caring and maybe more . . .

When she gets to the excitement stage, Roger's first reaction is more shock. He has been withholding his anger all these years in order to be liked and not rejected or abandoned (the child's decision). Now he discovers that bringing out his anger gets a response exactly the *opposite* of what he has been expecting all these years. In fact, he gets the response he was expecting as he withheld his anger. He begins to understand that just maybe he doesn't have to be the good boy all the time in order to be loved. He gets to experience the excitement of trying out something new. He gets to experience the relief that comes when some blocked anger energy is moved. He gets to experience direct feedback that his partner wasn't harmed by his anger—in fact, quite the opposite. He gets to experience that, now, as an adult, he is fully capable of being with his powerful feelings in a boundaried way (without having to kill them altogether).

Choosing to Live with Anger as an Adult

Valerie and Roger have a long way to go yet in their anger training, but they have made the first breakthrough, a start that wouldn't have happened unless they had the courage to try out some direct experience of moving feelings. Now they need to learn how to become a little more comfortable with powerful energies of anger. The main part of this stage is simply practice. Like unused physical muscles, these emotional muscles will be stiff at first. Practice and refine, practice and refine some more. They need to continue discovering that a direct experience of feelings will take them more places as individuals and as a couple than talking-about feelings could ever do.

Here's the choice: You can stay in a child's place about anger (which means avoiding it or expressing it in passive or unboundaried ways), or you can develop an adult capacity to express and receive anger. When Valerie said early on she wanted someone who would match her feelings, she was really saying she wanted a man who could deal with anger, rather than a boy who hides from it. A man who is emotionally his age knows his boundaries, and he knows that anger, in its place, is part of an authentic, responsible masculinity. He also knows that a real man must learn how to receive a woman's anger (only a boy would run or reflexively need to defend). For her part, an emotionally mature woman knows that anger is just part of who she is and there are times when it needs to come forth. The child part of her has difficulty when a man's anger comes her way, but the woman inside can be with it.

The choice, as always, is yours.

6

When Men
Don't Feel

Most people, men in particular, have difficulty with feelings and are resistant to learning more about them. Like it or not, feelings skills are the building blocks of intimate relating. It follows that if we want our second marriages to be all they can be, we have to overcome our resistance and open up to feelings. It's either that or forget about sustaining a passionate relationship. So many first marriages have failed over this issue we believe it is worth addressing one more time.

A Lesson for Men

The woman's voice: When we are starved for emotional nourishment because our partner refuses to give it, we first feel *disappointed,* then *disillusioned,* and eventually we will *complain* a lot and become *angry.* Finally, because our primary needs are not being met, we are likely to want to *retaliate.* How? Probably by refusing to meet our partner's primary needs. If this kind of relating continues for years, we are likely to get seriously *depressed,* feel *hopeless,* and go *numb.* We may even turn to eating or addictive behavior to try to relieve our experience of emotional starvation. However it unfolds, one thing is certain: The eventual outcome is that we will *turn off* to our partner. Sooner or later, the gutsier ones of us will be out the door and ready to take the risk of finding something or someone more nourishing. Others of us will go dead, become *nags*, find *affairs*, *withdraw* into ourselves, or exit in some other way.

Understanding Women

We couldn't count the number of times we have heard variations of that voice. Although men and women can be on either side of the feelings equation, in our experience it is generally the male partner who does not take the problem seriously. He balks at doing anything about it, and is often shocked when the crisis that has been rumbling under the surface for years finally comes out in full force. Even then, the guy is often reluctant to feel his feelings and can spend a great deal of his energy in defiance, judging his partner as "irrational," unpredictable, or impossible to please. He acts out the victim role when, in fact, he has played a significant role in creating the dilemma that is now in front of him. He was not being intentionally dense; he just didn't open his eyes enough to see things from her viewpoint.

Okay, men, let's just step into her shoes for a moment and follow this through again. Stretch yourself and imagine *you* are the Feelings person, the woman, and *you* are involved with a head-type person. Here you are with all of this churning, vibrating body experience. Energy is coursing through your body. You have all kinds of feelings and you are tingling, alive. It makes no difference what the nature of the particular feeling is or whether you happen to like it. Some of them you welcome, some you aren't so willing to have, but you experience feelings as part of what it is to be alive—and you are living.

You found your way to a mate. In the beginning he gave you passion, mainly in the form of his desire, his sexuality, his wanting. It didn't matter so much what his particular feelings were; the fact was that *they were his feelings*, they were out there, and they felt good to you. He seemed to be full of energy and

excitement. He shared his inner world of feelings with enthu-
siasm, or at least gave promise that he would.

Now, however, some of the excitement has worn off. You've
made a commitment and you are working at creating a life together. You still have lots of feelings, but the man you're with
has changed. He has become more outer-oriented. He lives in
his head more than his gut. Now when you bring things up,
you tend to get philosophy and advice. Either that or you get
silence. Sometimes, you get ignored. You get criticism—some
overt, some unspoken—but even if it is unspoken, you get it
anyway. From time to time, you get told how you should feel.
You don't get much in the way of feelings from him, which
means you don't get much from his heart.

Some of the philosophy you get is good and adds to your
awareness, though a lot is based merely on theories and ideas,
coming from someone who has not experienced life at any
greater depth than you have. Much of the "philosophy" is
based on idealistic notions about how life ought to be, and is
not particularly well grounded in the guts of living. Further,
while you find that this rational and analytical maneuvering is
often applied by him to you, very little of it is applied by him
to himself!

The advice can be helpful at times, but it has become
strangely annoying. And there's a reason why you are annoyed.
On the surface, the act of advice-giving is usually well-
intended, but it has a darker side. When one probes beneath
the surface, one usually discovers that the advice-giver is unconsciously assuming a position of greater power relative to the
person who is receiving this counsel. He gets comfort from
being in this position. The advice-giver, who is very caught up
in the words he is offering, is usually entirely oblivious to the
way he finds *feelings* of power by assuming the role of teacher.
But, sooner or later, the lowly receiver of the advice always gets
the picture. An urgency to dish out advice also interrupts the
process of legitimate discovery, which can be very annoying to
someone who is seeking true insight into the nature of life and
personal experience.

So here you are: The one who *feels*, on the receiving end of philosophy, discourses, and advice (much of it unsolicited). Interestingly, in exchanges with this Thinking partner, somehow the one who needs to be "fixed" usually turns out to be *you*. As a Feelings type, you may appreciate these gems of wisdom, but from this intimate human relationship, you want something more personal than philosophy and advice. You want your partner to go beyond platitudes and give you something from *inside* himself. He is, after all, supposed to be the closest person in the world to you.

You go along with this for a while, but finally you find yourself sinking a little. Your own Feelings nature tends to bog down when it is judged, "fixed," deemed defective. Your ability to respond nimbly and joyfully to the life-force slows. You begin to feel heavier.

You also begin to notice that you don't get a lot that's especially personal, that you can really get your teeth into. In fact, when the personal issues between the two of you get challenging, your partner tends to withdraw—if not physically, then certainly into the world of his own mind or perhaps the world of his work. He *thinks* he is present, but you are not able to *feel* him or get any kind of "felt" energy from him. It's like standing next to an empty shell. You have a hard time telling what his inner experience is. And why should you care? *Because he is your life partner, and you really want to know what is happening inside of him.*

More time goes by. The feelings and energies are still coursing through your veins. You'd like more life out of your partner, more contact with him, more of his inner world. By now, you don't even care so much if what you get is wonderful or horrible. You just want *something*. Because you're a feeler, putting precise words on what you need is hard, but what you are certain of is this: you are hoping for more. You may even cry out. What you do get? Defensiveness. Resistance. Quizzical looks, like you must be crazy. He might take your wish for deepened contact as a personal attack. You get fancy words turned around against you. Occasionally you get signs of his wanting to participate more, but seldom any significant and lasting action.

Now you start to get angry. You can see the situation clearly. You *feel* it clearly. What you want for yourself will also be good for your partner. Your desires are not something you are self-ishly insisting on. What you want is to enhance the whole re-lationship. You don't need 100 percent of everything right now. You're willing to settle for just an indication of some move-ment. It is not that big a deal. All you want is something a lit-tle more real and personal, now and again. Your instinct tells you that even a small breakthrough into your feeling-world by your partner could set the whole relationship on a new road. It would make such a difference if, maybe five to ten times, each week, you got an "I feel . . ." statement from this person you deeply care for and love—a statement in which the blank is filled in with a *real feeling*. But what do you get instead? More stubborn resistance. Somebody who feels personally criticized by your expression of a need and is therefore resisting you at every turn. It's maddening.

When bits of your anger emerge, your partner tells you not to be angry—it's inappropriate, off-course, a distraction, a dis-ruption, not safe. Anger is wrong, you are told. Philosophically speaking, there ought only to be harmony, gentleness, and un-conditional love in this relationship (and, from his point of view, *you* ought to be providing more of it). Nope, no anger: Don't need it, don't want it, don't want to get it, don't want to give it. Rational people ought to be above anger. He can rise above it. If you can't, you must be defective.

There isn't really very much juice in all this. Actually, it is kind of dull. Sometimes you even push for a reaction, any kind of reaction, just to get something happening! Except for your experience together in the bedroom or the sudden appearance of a catastrophe, like an accident or a death in the family, you have to push too hard to get some feeling energy back. You begin to recognize that your own life-force is diminishing; you recognize that some of that is because you don't feel like you used to. Not just toward him, but within yourself, about yourself. You find yourself increasingly reluctant to bring out your energy. The jewels you have to offer are not being welcomed. But, you don't want to give up on this marriage. So what can you do?

A new idea! You suggest therapy, which—done right—includes at least some training in feeling awareness. And what do you get?

- "Therapists are all screwed up themselves. Why should I go to one of them?" (Translation: "No.")
- "A therapist? We don't have *those* kinds of problems. Maybe you think we do, but I don't. In fact, I'm pretty happy with things the way they are." (Translation: "No.")
- "Not enough money, not enough time." (Translation: "No.")
- This is just a bunch of woman-speak. I resent and reject demands from you for me to be *like* you; one woman in this relationship is enough. I will be my own person." ("No.")
- "I'll think about it . . . " (Really a defensive move: a week later no evidence of following through has shown up. "No.")
- "How come it always has to be your way? ("No.")
- And so forth . . .

Now, as a Feelings person, one who needs feelings—some juice, some energy—you reflect on these statements you've heard over the years. What you are hearing is resistance, excuses, defiance, defensiveness, a child looking for and expecting a good mommy, whiny man-as-victim stuff. Sugar-coated or rationalized, gently explained or abrasively defended, these responses all add up to "*No.*" They all add up to your being with a partner who doesn't place a very high priority on you and your needs. All in all, it is pretty discouraging—one might even say pathetic. You know, beneath all of these words, he has emotions and is basically afraid of his emotional being, but he won't even come clean about that.

Now, Thinking person: How would life be for you if you were this Feelings person—asking for something essential to you and getting these types of answers? Imagine yourself as a Feelings person whose partner not only refuses to come forth with his feelings, but won't accept yours, either. That's not quite accurate. What he really wants are your "positive" feelings when they are convenient for him, and he wants very little of your so-called "negative" feelings (that is, those that are not agreeable to him).

Imagine being with a Thinking person who wants your energy and aliveness as a companion, which obviously has a lot to do with your feelings, then a little later wants to squash or rationalize away your feelings because they are not convenient to him. He wants your sex but doesn't want (and, in fact, won't accept) your anger. He wants you to be "happy" but won't attend to your primary needs. He wants your "up" feelings and tries to "fix" (which means "get rid of") your "down" feelings. He talks of and worries about not being accepted by you, but routinely rejects your feelings (which are, after all, *you*)—and is scarcely aware that he is doing it!

Why Do Men Resist Learning about Feelings?

It's ironic. A man is taught that he will get respect by controlling his feelings. He spends years developing the capacity to do this. Then, in his primary relationship, with probably the one person in the world from whom he most deeply desires respect, he *loses* respect as a result of the things he did to gain respect. This, to put it gently, does not make a lot of sense. So how is a man to deal with his dilemma?

To begin, he can understand that rational thinking is grounded in an either/or mode of cognition. Thus the Thinking type person implicitly accepts this underlying premise: It is either my way (mind-based) *or* her way (feeling-based). Not a little bit of my way and a little bit of her way, but my way *or* her way. If there is a choice between the two, I must of course hold onto my way, lest I be defeated or humiliated. If I open to her way, I will be giving up something of fundamental value for me, perhaps even sacrificing my masculine essence. If feelings are as they appear to be, which is weakness, and my way is one of strength—strength being good while weakness is bad—I must hold onto my position in order to retain my power and integrity.

Now this type of thinking might be all right for a younger mind at a certain developmental stage of life, a mind trying to take its initial sightings on the vastness of reality by sifting everything into two simple categories. But it is a very limited approach and scarcely suited for carrying into even a first marriage, much less a second. A mature mind must be able to see broader vistas and be capable of holding many different perspectives at one time, which includes being able to discern the simultaneous value of both the rational and the feeling aspects of life. The authentically mature man must have access to both.

Most men and women have come into adulthood defending against their feelings to some degree because it is an adaptive strategy for coping. Feelings expose our vulnerability and, at certain younger stages, allowing vulnerability is too threatening. Holding powerful emotions in our bodies takes a solid container and younger bodies are not well enough equipped. Pushing away from feelings was a great strategy, but there was a cost. We learned to operate primarily in just one dimension of ourselves, that of the mind, when two were available. And then, by using our minds to justify continuing this mind-only strategy, we fooled ourselves into thinking we were whole. But while we can fool ourselves, we can't fool the partners with whom we live in intimate relationship, or the kids we raise, who are profoundly affected by our one-sidedness. (Children generally aren't able to articulate their need for their father's feelings until later in life. Then, although remedial work can still take place, the effect of a father's absent feelings has taken its toll.)

It is sad that so many men get polarized against their partner when she calls out for feelings. They consider it some sort of attack from the feminine, not recognizing it for what it is: a plea for their men to be all they can be, as whole in their masculinity as they can be. Men can only gain by bringing more awareness to their feelings. It is not a matter of losing; it's a matter of *adding* to oneself.

Doug's Story: Man to Man

The realm of feelings is difficult territory for most men—even therapists. We want to depart from our author partnership for a moment and allow Doug to speak to men directly:

As a man, I know what it is like to struggle with feelings. After a dozen years of immersion in the territory, I *still* struggle. I suspect that I always *will* struggle. Clearly, the problem is not a matter of whether I *have* feelings or not. Rather, it is that my feelings are often hard for me to locate and even harder for me to express.

To be completely honest, if I could have things the way I want them, I wouldn't volunteer to spend a lot of my time developing feelings skills. I haven't met a man who would. Contacting feelings takes considerable ongoing effort. I have spent a lifetime developing rational skills, and I would much rather relate to the rest of the world from a position that reflects my strength, rather than one that reflects something with which I have, in general, had little practice. And doing that is much easier if I stay in my head.

All that would be fine if I chose to live as a single man. I've watched many men attempt to live in a marriage like the single men they once were, and have yet to see even one of them contented with what he gets back from his partner. It's wanting the best of both worlds and it doesn't work. (Oh, it might work all right with docile, subservient women who have been taught their mission is to serve men, but there is a cost there as well—one I wouldn't pay.)

A man who wants fulfilling intimacy with a vital woman over the long term must be able to meet her primary needs and find ways to get his own needs met. This is just common sense: *Each* person's primary needs must be met in order for a relationship between them to be successful. When one's own primary needs are consistently met, a desire to give to the other person just follows naturally. No loss of self needs to occur in this act.

Here's an important idea to grasp. *Feelings in relationship are a primary need for a woman.* There is no "right" or "wrong" about this need. It's just how things are. For women, feelings are like food; and without some feelings in their relationship, they end up with a sensation not unlike that of starvation. It is just that basic for women. Furthermore, whether she is consciously aware of it or not, a woman experiences the movement of feelings as akin to the movement of life-energy, and if she is unable to move her feelings (and be with a person who is able to move his), the net effect is similar to that of choking off the circulation of that life energy in her. When a slowing of her life energy occurs, the net result is a person who is less than fully alive, and with that energy slowed for long enough, a person who is numb . . . to her partner and to life itself.

Recently, we received a note from a man who did some feelings training with us a while back. He was a physician and very well trained mentally, but he was having difficulty with his marriage. He wrote, "Primarily important in marriage is to keep the relationship alive. And I know now that involves staying alive myself." This simple comment captures an essential truth from a man who was ready to take on more responsibility. He was finally hearing the message his partner had been delivering to him for a number of years.

Stepping Back to Move Forward

If you are serious about developing your capacity to experience feelings, it will be necessary to go back to where growth in that area stopped. Since your emotional self was probably shut off many years ago, to open up that area again requires you to acknowledge that you have some catching up to do, that emotionally you are younger (and in some ways perhaps *much* younger) than your chronological age.

A man's challenge with the emotional realms is not the result of a built-in defect or of insurmountable conditioning. It is just a matter of his having focused habitually away from his inner nature—probably for his entire life. And the solution simply involves retraining, becoming more alert, applying oneself to learning a new skill. The first stumbling block is in getting started; next it is a matter of summoning the will to stay with it long enough to get to the rewards.

Men are sometimes rather short of stamina when it comes to feelings training. After some initial success, they tend to let go of the effort. We see it all the time in our groups. Men come in terrified of being in a group that's involved in emotional learning. But, with a little help and encouragement, they get a good start at locating, expressing, and receiving feelings. They are amazed to discover through direct experience what it is like to be more present in their bodies. (They gain some comfort when they discover that their wives also have a lot to learn about expressing and receiving feelings.) They are shocked at how quickly their wives perk up and how juicy the relationship gets in relatively short order. With a few feelings out and the juices flowing again, the men leave the group thinking the "problem is solved." Great! Then they pull their attention away from their feelings, fall back into old habits, and wonder why the relationship heads toward dryness again.

Working to be multidimensional after spending decades honing just one dimension is obviously not something that is finished overnight. Deeply ingrained patterns of relating don't change easily. After the initial breakthroughs, partners might discover that at least six months of continued effort are required to implement the feeling basics. Beyond that, continuing effort is still required. And if one or both of the partners forgets what's been learned (which often happens under stress), the tendency will always be to go back to what is known and long-practiced: leading with the mind. There is no quick fix here, which probably explains why so few people take the challenge seriously on an ongoing basis.

We hear a lot—particularly from men who have not done this type of training—about how this feeling stuff is for soft males, and fierceness is what masculinity is about. Yes, fierceness and courage in the outer realms is important, but a man without a corresponding courage to explore his inner realms is still only half a man. Any man who has been through some feelings training can attest to the fact that it is anything but soft work. In fact, many of them have never sweat so much in their lives! And none of them lost one bit of their masculinity in the process.

The Bottom Line

Men can't get the best out of their relationships with women unless they are willing to develop their feeling selves more fully. If they want passion with their partner, they have to be willing to supply feelings—women can't be expected to carry the whole load. Men who want their own primary needs met have to meet their partner's primary needs in return. Men who want to raise well-balanced, emotionally healthy children must be able to provide a balanced, whole, authentic masculine— *and that includes feelings*. (I wish every man could spend time witnessing the difference in emotional health between children raised by fathers who were, at least somewhat, in touch with feelings and by fathers who were not.)

Men often develop the attitude that having feelings and expressing them equals weakness. In intimacy, just the opposite is true. In an intimate relationship, a man who cannot express his anger in a clear and clean way is really just a covered-over boy. The same is true of a man who can't receive a woman's anger. A man who looks to his partner to set the emotional tone in his relationship because he has not explored his own emotional capabilities sufficiently is weak. He doesn't have his full resources available to him and will ultimately be perceived by his partner as crippled in some way. A man who dies early because he has frozen over his feelings is a sacrifice, not a hero. The demand for feelings is not some kind of anti-male conspiracy; it is a prayer for men to discover and bring forth the best that they can be.

7

The Dark Side
of Mothering

As partners distance themselves from their feelings, they tend to adopt certain roles or habitual postures in relation to each other. Each of those roles becomes automatic and is accompanied by a limited, constricting pattern of behavior. As we've seen, men tend to drop the ball by going to their heads and want to relate primarily from the rational, analytical, abstracted part of themselves. Women often opt for the role of "mother" to their partner. The impact is profound. In fact, as women spend more and more time in this role, they become just as emotionally unavailable to their partners as men do when they take refuge in their heads.

Will Mother Make It Better?

Women have been prepared by centuries of biological and psychological evolution, as well as by lifelong cultural, social, and family influences, to nurture and instruct developing human beings from infancy to emerging adulthood. But when this behavior is focused on another adult, particularly on a woman's intimate partner, there will be trouble.

Mother wants to protect and make things "safe." She wants everything to be in harmony and everyone to be fed, physically and emotionally. She wants to "make it all better" for everyone. Mother is also a teacher of life—and she watches, comments frequently, and can be very critical of what she sees (especially with regard to her primary adult charge: her partner!). In order to accomplish *all* these tasks (and though she might like to pretend otherwise), *she needs to have control.*

The multidimensional Mother in many other world traditions—exemplified by Kali and Durga in India and Asia, for example—includes other aspects alongside the nurturer. This archetypal Mother can also be destructive, righteously angry, and fury-filled, a balancing force for masculine energy. She cuts through illusion and gets directly to the truth. A far cry from the one-dimensional Mother type we know, a sweetened, idealized image of harmony and goodness.

Nurturing new growth means cutting away the dead wood as well as watering the seeds. In order to access their *genuinely* powerful nature, women need to develop these more challenging aspects of the feminine ideal.

Women gravitate toward the role of mother for a very good reason: In our mixed-up culture, with its confusion about femininity, Mother is the one aspect of women that is widely accepted as powerful, worthy, virtuous, and beyond reproach. In a young woman's mind, Mother becomes equated with what the adult, mature, well-developed feminine surely must be. So when she is married, wanting to be the most powerful feminine she can be, she is strongly tempted to take that role on with a vengeance. As her marriage progresses, if she feels powerless relative to her partner, bolstering up her mother self is a way of hiding from that.

If Mother were taking her turn with all the other parts of the feminine, there wouldn't be a major problem. But, in many first marriages, that is not what happens. Mother has a tendency to take over the entire stage and refuse to get off! As a consequence, other parts of a woman's feminine nature don't get a chance to grow—and unbridled Mother has a deadly effect on intimate relating.

In fact, women who get stuck in the Mother role create just as many difficulties in their relationships as men who are separated from their feelings. From our experience, it takes about the same amount of effort for a woman to leave the Mother role as it takes for a man to learn about feelings. And women who are stuck in the Mother role are just as oblivious to their contribution to the breakdown of their marriages as unfeeling men.

The Mother-Role Run Amok

Let's drop in on a relationship sometime after the first major commitment has been made. The courtship is over, and the time has come for both partners to get to work making a life together. Because they're human and living in a complex world, they have insecurities, fears, and parts of themselves they would rather not acknowledge. Men, as we have seen, tend to become Thinking types as a way of coping. Women, seeking a balancing power, become Mothers.

Initially, this role feels good—take-charge, womanly, the right thing to be and do. As the man, by acting out of his intellect, bolsters his view of himself as a powerful masculine person, she bolsters herself as a powerful feminine person. But there are costs to her as a person and as an intimate partner.

Let's start with the costs to herself. The Perfect Mother is superwoman who takes care of one and all, perhaps in addition to earning a living. She sacrifices her own needs to the well-being of others, and has endless energy to do so. The trouble is, sooner or later, the real woman wakes up and becomes very unhappy about this self-induced sacrifice. She is justifiably angry; but since "good mothers don't get angry," the anger is suppressed. She feels like exploding, but good mothers don't do that either. Good mothers don't complain, so a lot of feelings get stuffed. Such an angry, unhappy, unsatisfied, and frustrated woman does not a good partner make!

A woman who gets caught up in being Mother *believes* she is fully present to herself and to others, but she is not. The same is generally true for anyone who makes the well-being of others their top priority. Healers, rescuers, and saviors get a sense of personal identity and worthiness by attending to others, and that's fine. But people who start overdeveloping this role early in life and live the major part of their life doing and being for others, often don't get the chance to know who *they* really are inside themselves. After many years of this, when the Mother type takes enough time to slow down and feel (which is not all that often), big feelings of emptiness often come welling up. Underneath her cover, she doesn't really know who she is.

The woman who adopts the Mother role in a big way needs to have control. When we look more deeply into this character, we discover a person who has not the slightest bit of confidence that anyone would ever be capable of looking after her if she ever let her control, her Mother self, down. She is convinced she has to work very hard and carry the whole load herself. She *has to take control* because she believes that no one cares like she does—and no one else is as competent. It's a recipe for exhaustion.

Mother is expected to be a giver, and give she does. The trouble is, in her rush to pick up the Mother mantle, she didn't stop to ask herself a very important question: How can someone who hasn't learned how to receive from others give much of anything that is real? To put it another way: How can partners who are only playing a role, and not truly at home inside, give that which is truly valuable to their intimates? Empty, unhappy, depleted individuals can only go through the motions of giving, through the act of doing. They are not able to give from within their inner selves, their deeper being, their fuller presence.

A woman in the Mother role goes through the motions of giving and tries her hardest to do what is right. But as she gives from a place that is one-dimensional, from a place of "shoulds," those closest to her see her as going through the motions rather than doing something with real heart behind it. In large part, Mother doesn't get appreciated for her efforts, which leads to an even bigger sense of emptiness as the years go by.

Eventually, Mother becomes a woman who has run herself down and doesn't get appreciated for it. She is absorbed in the lives of those who are in her charge, and distanced from her inner self. She has been so involved with wearing the mask of Mother she doesn't really know who she is.

In some ways, being Mother is very safe. It doesn't require much in the way of personal vulnerability, and (until she exhausts herself with it) it gives her feelings of power and efficacy. Playing this role also evokes a certain sense of righteousness; and even though its rewards aren't very satisfying over the long run, this righteousness justifies an air of superiority and a presumed authority. She holds herself as the one who knows best. From the Mother position, it is easy to point the finger at the partner for any difficulties in intimacy. And that leads us to the biggest problem of Mother as mate.

Mother as Mate

A Mother, by definition, does not see her partner as a man, but as a son. In the earlier stages of marriage, she didn't see him this way. But now, as she really grows into the Mother role, he seems more and more in need of her care. After all, Mother is the source and all life stems from her. From this secret attitude, her husband-son needs to be instructed about life. By holding to this attitude, she always gets to place herself one-up in relation to him. If her partner is not a man but a "boy," then she gets to play it safe by secretly blaming him for many of the problems that arise between them. She is the mature one, the one who sacrifices, and the one who is above reproach. Nothing is Mother's fault.

The defense structure she forms around this role is every bit as tight as the defense structure of the man who sees everything rationally, from his mind. Behind her role she is almost untouchable. She sees her son-partner out of touch with his emotions; but within her role, she doesn't see how she is every bit as unavailable. She sees how he protects his inner self from her (and she knows what it feels like to be on the receiving end of that), but she cannot see how she protects her inner self from him. Her partner's defiance is clear to her, but she cannot see how she is equally determined to hold onto her position of safety.

The Mother tells herself she wants a man, not a boy (but for some reason never chooses one). After a number of years in her marriage, she gets quite disgusted with her partner, who invariably ends up disappointing her. It is almost impossible for her to see the cause and effect: that by locking her vision on him as a boy, that is what she gets. The more a woman acts out Mother, the more she gets Son in return. Of course, she prefers to see this drama of his son-like behavior entirely as a shortcoming of his (as if he has regressed during their time together, while she somehow has grown). Not being conscious of her own narrow viewpoint, she doesn't see that she has any responsibility in the problem at all. Just as her feeling-challenged partner is unaware of his role in creating the lack of passion, she is unaware of her contribution to the emotional dullness in her marriage.

How Her Mate Sees Mother

Let's step into the shoes of a man whose intimate partner has taken on the Mother role. In the beginning of the relationship, things were great. She was open and sexual; she saw the powerful man in him and was willing to surrender to that, at least now and then. The Mother part of her that surfaced occasionally was welcome (it showed she cared), just as some fathering from him was welcome (it showed he cared). After the commitment, though, things began to change. She got a lot more serious. Ever so gradually, she became much more controlling. And then there is this secret attitude of hers: All men are boys, or more specifically, he is one. Maybe she comes out openly about it or maybe she doesn't, but he starts feeling as if she sees him as incompetent and untrustworthy in some very deep way. He may not be in immediate contact with these feelings, but he gets the idea. "Mother" watches his movements. "Mother" is trying to figure him out—maybe even with a bit of suspicion. "Mother" tries to poke and pry into his life. "Mother" has an uncanny knack of telling him what he needs to do . . . just the moment before he was going to do it anyway.

In the first few years, she might have bitten her lip, but as time has gone by, she has become more openly critical. The things he does for her aren't usually all that well recognized, because the mother part of her is not such a great receiver. But the things he *doesn't* do to her specifications are certainly recognized, and they come under major scrutiny. He has his own way of doing things, but somehow it comes through that *her* way is the right way and that's all there is to it (in her mind). Further, her attitude says she really doesn't trust him to come through, certainly not without her pushing. It wears on him and makes him not want to try so hard.

When you give one of your feelings to a woman who is in her "Mother" role, she is likely to come crashing in on top of you. Mothers are often in a rush. She wants to know this and that, what is going on, how to fix it, and so forth. Sometimes she grabs your feeling and runs with it like a fullback, straight-arming downfield, often heading to all manner of places you never intended to go. It gets you to thinking that you better consider twice before offering another feeling!

With Mother hanging over you, you quite naturally want some space now and again, someplace where you can have things your way, at your pace, without any questioning or criticism (the "cave," they call it these days). However, a woman who is in the Mother role is apt to take this need of yours as a personal affront to her. She does all this sacrificing for *you* and you don't want to be around *her!* (The truth is that the Mother part of a woman is terrified of being on her own because her very existence depends on doing and being for others.)

She talks a good game about feelings, but much of the time she is numb. She is usually very focused on you but doesn't truly offer much of her personal vulnerability. Most of the time you only see the controlled and controlling Mother—until, all of a sudden without much warning, a dam bursts somewhere and she gets blown off the stage accompanied by a torrent of feelings. Now, you can take one feeling at a time, or even a few; but when a giant tidal wave of emotion hits, you can't really do much other than to head for safer ground.

Approaching her about any of this is hard, because as she sits in the very righteous position of Mother, she is in a huge defense herself. On the surface, she appears more open, and as a woman she might actually be a little more open than you are, but the truth is she isn't all *that* open (especially to you). She thinks she is far more present than you are, but you feel as deprived of her juicy presence as she is starved for your emotional presence. Any way you look at it, it's not a very exciting relationship. And because you don't know how to change things, you tend to withdraw.

And Then a Child Arrives

The Mother role may not be too noticeable at the beginning of a relationship, but after the first baby arrives, it can really take off. Before she had a baby, Mother would get offstage now and again so the other parts of her womanness could stretch a bit and have some fun. Now she *really is* a mother, and the woman-mother part of her hardly *ever* gets offstage. All the things that came up before now get amplified by several orders of magnitude.

Mother in the Bedroom

Mother isn't really into sex. Orgasms don't come easily to her. Other parts of her feminine nature have far more interest in sex, but if Mother is on the stage all the time they don't get much of a chance. And this is particularly true if the Mother part has been so busy mothering actual children that there isn't much energy left in the body system. The sexual part of her marriage inevitably drops down in priority.

Mothers don't have sex for themselves. If they do it at all, they do it for their partners. A woman who is having sex for her partner and not for herself eventually ends up feeling resentful and used. Sex is the one area of intimacy that requires two people who can be at home in their bodies, and Mother isn't really home.

For her husband, having sex with Mother presents a problem: A son having sex with his mother is not the way it is supposed to be. His psyche is going to signal him to avoid sex altogether, or to get in and out as quickly as possible.

She Flees to Mother,
He Flees to His Mind

There are a lot of parallels between a woman's flight to her Mother role and a man's flight to his Thinking role. Even though each partner is convinced he or she is fully present, in truth, neither one is. Both are present on the surface, but neither is available with their deeper feeling selves for intimate relating. He seeks refuge in his mind and she seeks refuge in her role; neither has to experience much vulnerability in those places. Just as he has separated from parts of himself and gone to a place that is safer for him, so has she. Both then have a strong tendency to define themselves in terms of what they *do*, as opposed to who they are inside, underneath their outside presentation.

We must remember that each person's position or role serves a very valid purpose initially. The roles help each partner to locate and occupy an identity within the relationship, which is an important task at the beginning. Leaping headfirst into a lifelong commitment is something few of us are fully equipped to deal with (even the second time around). Having an identity that supports our legitimate needs for power and efficacy helps to keep us from getting lost or overwhelmed by the enormity of the experience. Getting stuck in the roles long-term, however, causes serious trouble for the relationship. A man locked into his head with a woman committed completely to her role as mother, dries up the intimacy quickly.

The Way In Is the Way Out

If the Mother role or a Thinking-only mind-set has taken too big a space in your marriage, you might remind yourself that roles and mind-sets, no matter how thoroughly ingrained, are merely habits, and habits can be broken. The way out begins by mustering the will to look inward.

Both partners must first observe their own tendencies to narrow themselves into roles. This is a big step. Individuals, while active in their chosen role or mind-sets, can claim to see all that needs to be seen. Partners can help cue us, but when we are stuck inside a role, it is tough to hear the message. Having been through a marriage or two, let's hope we don't have to let things get to a crisis point before we are willing to expand our repertoires.

The fastest way to shift out of roles is for partners to tune into their feelings at the very moment these roles are taking over. As soon as Mother expresses what she is really feeling, she is no longer Mother. She has entered the woman behind the role. As soon as a man brings up his feelings he is no longer locked in his mind-set. It's a very simple answer but oh-so-hard to do in real life.

Both the woman caught in Mother and the man caught in Thinking have all manner of worthwhile, expansive, and exciting feelings underneath their protective coverings. In fact, it's beneath the roles where the passion lies. Talking about getting to that passion is a lot easier than doing what it takes—and you must decide if you are willing to take on the challenge.

PART 3

Issues of the Second Marriage: Exes, Children, and Money

8

Invisible Bonds: Living with Ex-Spouses

If we lived in a nice, tidy world, a legal divorce would sever all attachments between ex-spouses and that would be that. Both partners would be free to start over fresh and new, without any history to encumber them. However, we all know it doesn't work that way. After the divorce, ex-partners who have been together many years don't just un-merge completely at the stroke of a pen. Invisible threads of connection often remain intact. If they have not made a significant, conscious effort at ending the marriage (and we mean more than just letting the lawyers battle it out), unresolved feelings can persist for years afterward. It doesn't even matter what the feelings are: An attachment can be maintained just as much by unresolved hostility and anger as it can be by love and affection.

In a second marriage, one partner's leftover attachments to an ex-spouse can destroy the new relationship. Why? Because when there are three or more players in the marriage, it is not possible for a husband and wife to reach full potential in intimacy with each other. These leftover attachments interfere with setting the foundation in the new relationship. Furthermore, because these bonds are not tangible, many new partners are not aware of how attached they still are to their exes—and they usually don't particularly want to know, either.

The partner with the attachment is generally unaware that he or she is not bringing all of himself or herself into the new marriage. *But the new partner always senses it.* The new partner, being powerfully invested in the outcome of this new relationship and extremely attentive to what's going on, quickly senses the unresolved bond that still exists. Sooner or later, the new partner challenges the attached partner about leftover bonds. The attached partner almost invariably denies it, and the friction begins.

If nothing happens to diminish the strength of the leftover bonding, abrasive dialogues in the second marriage become more common. Essentially, the new partner begins pushing for resolution, usually in the form of demanding less contact between the attached partner and the ex. The attached partner refuses to acknowledge the problem and resists changing the situation. As tension builds, the new partner is often labeled as controlling and insecure. The attached partner is judged as blind to what is really going on. Control struggles may follow over whose perception is "right." The specifics might vary somewhat, but one thing can't be denied, with a phantom partner in the middle, the optimum potential for intimacy in the second marriage can't be realized.

Ann and Mike: Holding On

Ann and Mike have been married about a year and a half. Generally, things have been going well between them, but one issue stubbornly resists any attempt at resolution. It has to do with Ann's continuing relationship with her ex-spouse, Daniel.

Ann and Daniel were together ten years. During that time they had the usual ups and downs, but their partnership just didn't have the passion either of them had hoped for. The way they summed it up: "Neither of us was at fault, really; things just ran their course and came to an end." The split was a long time in coming, but it was relatively pain-free. Both felt pride that they were able to remain good friends after the divorce.

When Ann spoke of her intent to keep a friendship with Daniel, Mike viewed it as a little out of the ordinary (it certainly didn't go that way with *his* ex) but not as any particular threat to him. He assumed their friendship would fade over time. Mike knew that Daniel was the nice-guy type who liked to remain friends with many women, and Mike expected that he would gradually find a life of his own.

It didn't turn out that way. After a few months, Daniel's frequent contact with Ann started to make Mike feel uncomfortable. He thought, "I'm her new mate and I'm willing to bring all of myself into this, but part of her is still back with her ex. How can I move along and go deeper into this marriage when she won't?" Mike became more vocal about wanting Ann to reduce contact with Daniel.

She resisted. Ann thought Mike's attitude stemmed from an out-dated turf-guarding instinct, and she resented his attempt to control her friendships. In this enlightened age, she declared, a friendship between a married woman and a single man ought to be possible. She had been friends with Daniel before she even knew Mike, and she couldn't understand why they couldn't stay friends now.

Both Ann and Mike seem to have defensible positions, but a wedge is forming between them over this issue. Clearly—at least to Mike—Ann still has some kind of attachment to her ex and doesn't want to let go. Mike senses that she is not fully committed to him, and that makes him uncomfortable.

Ann and Mike are at a standoff. What don't they know that might help them get clearer? Or perhaps we could ask, what's going on outside their awareness?

Just Good Friends?

Staying friends with an ex-spouse is a grand ideal. Over the long term, after the new marriage has become very firmly established, it may even genuinely develop in that direction. But the desire to stay connected as friends with an ex can lead to a second marriage that isn't operating up to full potential. Let's take a peek at the shadow side of divorced partners who intend to remain good friends after the breakdown of their marriage.

In our work, we frequently observed that partners who have a very strong need to define themselves as "friends" after the pain of divorce very often had more of a brother-sister type of marriage than a man-woman marriage. Sometimes a brother-sister relationship is passionate in the very early stages, but fairly early on it begins to go flat. Partners relate well from their heads and sometimes their hearts, but neither feels safe with the deeper, more powerful feelings. Each partner comes to be seen by the other more as a caring sibling than as a lover.

This doesn't suggest that love isn't present, but rather that it is more of a familial love than a man-woman love. Partners in this sort of marriage eventually end up feeling stifled; neither partner feels able to achieve a more mature masculine or feminine persona within the relationship. They might bemoan their lack of passion (each often pointing the finger at the other as the "immature one," of course), but they have difficulty parting because the relationship meets core security needs, much as one's family of origin provides security needs in the earlier phases of life. Deep down, *both* partners know the bond is one of security rather than passionate fulfillment, but neither wants to admit it. Rather than acknowledge any of this to themselves, they just end up feeling frustrated.

When an individual has met this type of powerful security need for many years, that individual is very hard to let go of. In fact, brother and sister do not *want* to let go of each other completely. So, when the realization finally comes that they have reached the limit of where they can go together as a couple, they lessen the blow of separation by telling themselves they will remain friends. That way, both partners avoid the full pain of the divorce experience, the full pain of breaking away from a person who, in some deep way, has acted as a substitute family member.

In addition, by ending the marriage as "friends," partners collude in developing a kind of no-fault scenario. When neither partner is at fault, neither has to take personal responsibility for the failure of their experience together or for the difficulties that caused the breakdown. They can just smile and wave at each other at the last parting and tell themselves it was all for the best. Just as they hid from their deeper feelings when they were together, they hide from their deeper feelings on parting.

They Can't Have It All

This is what happened to Ann and her ex, Daniel. Theirs was a brother-sister marriage. In their resolve to part as friends (which was also a collusion to avoid feelings of pain and failure), neither really severed the energetic bond to the other. For Ann, this means that Daniel is still taking up some space in her heart, space that is not available to Mike. For Daniel, this means that he is not yet able to sustain an intimate bond with any woman.

How does holding onto her bond with Daniel serve Ann? We all have fears of diving headlong into intimacy with another, and this is one way for her to handle those fears. Hanging onto bonds from the past provides a measure of safety. Keeping one foot (or even a toenail) in the old camp means that she doesn't have to bring every part of her into the new camp. Keeping her bond with Daniel alive also means Ann doesn't have to take full responsibility for her efforts in the new marriage (she always has someone to fall back on if things get difficult).

The trouble is that Ann wasn't satisfied with Daniel as an intimate partner, and instinctively felt she needed another man in order to develop her more mature feminine nature. She made a commitment to Mike, but now she is withholding a full commitment to him. She won't move forward and she won't move backward—she is determined to hold onto the best of both worlds. But Mike will no longer go along with it, and no spouse worth having *would* do so.

Ann doesn't want to have any boundaries. She refuses to acknowledge what's true for all of us: that with all the demands on our time and attention, we have only a limited amount of energy for other people. When bonds still exist between past lovers or ex-spouses, we have that much *less* energy available for a new spouse (and family). When less energy is available for the new spouse, the possibilities for intimacy with the new spouse are diminished. Many people don't want to see it this way—preferring instead to believe they can have it all, old and new—but in real life, these folks usually find themselves short of the intimacy they desire.

Divorced partners need to invest considerable, focused time and effort on resolving any leftover feelings from their dead marriages before leaping in again. Find out who you were in the old marriage and examine the roles you played. When you jump into the new marriage too fast, as Ann seems to have done, you may secretly be looking for the easy path. Usually, however, you will end up paying a bigger price in the long run.

Even though Ann may prefer to believe she can have it all, she will ultimately need to make a decision. If she insists on holding onto Daniel, she is not committing fully to Mike; if she is not committing fully to Mike, she ends up with a diluted marriage. The truth is, marriage is tough and challenging enough without this kind of problem; many, many feelings will get in the way of intimacy. Starting it off by diluting the connection between herself and her husband (in order to keep contact with an ex-spouse) does not bode well for the new marriage. Sooner or later she'll have to make a choice.

Kevin and Joy: Paying Attention

Kevin and Joy are in their mid-thirties and have been married two years. They have no children. Kevin has been involved in starting up a new business from scratch and works long hours each day. Joy doesn't feel as if she is getting enough attention from him, and that's putting stress on the relationship. She tries to be understanding about it all, but something else really compounds the problem. Whenever Kevin's ex, Sally, calls, Kevin drops whatever he's doing to talk with her. Mostly he just listens, but sometimes he volunteers help.

At first Joy didn't want to be seen as the controlling wife-witch, so she let things go by as Kevin continued his contact with Sally. But when Joy started seeing how little attention *she* was getting from him, it began to annoy her. She and Kevin had increasingly bitter arguments over this issue, until Sally's calls finally seemed to diminish in frequency. Things calmed down for some time—until Joy discovered that Sally was calling Kevin at work instead of at home. Joy exploded, and demanded they seek counseling over this issue.

Kevin agreed that taking calls from Sally at work was a mistake, but he reported that he just got tired of Joy's nagging and all of the circular arguments over something he didn't see as being that important. Just because they weren't married anymore didn't mean he didn't care about Sally. They were together a lot of years and she was with him in some unique situations that only he and she are familiar with. Helping her out from time to time has been a natural instinct.

As Kevin sees it, Joy has become impossibly insecure. She is making this issue much bigger than it really is. He has explained with great deliberation to Joy that the relationship between him and Sally as romantic partners is finished. He has *many times* assured Joy of his love for her. Each day, he explains, he comes home exhausted, and all of this conflict about Sally during the precious moments when he is free at home is becoming too much for him.

Joy says that if Kevin is so concerned about his free time, he ought to consider cutting his time with Sally. She believes Sally has ulterior motives: Underneath her demure self-presentation, Sally secretly enjoys getting in the way of their marriage and proving the power she still has over Kevin. And the fact that Kevin was secretly in contact with her demonstrates that he is not as clean and clear about the situation as he thinks he is. Sally, claims Joy, is trying to disrupt their marriage—and she is succeeding. Kevin must cut his contact with her.

Kevin sees this demand as an all-out assault on his autonomy as a man. Joy is putting him into an impossible situation, and if he bends to her will on this, he will lose something of himself. As he sees it, the true answer to the problem is for Joy to develop a stronger sense of self so she won't be so threatened by this woman who is no threat.

What's Really Going On Here?

Kevin and Joy both have a piece of the truth. Kevin still has attachments he is not fully aware of; if he didn't have those attachments, Sally wouldn't be calling so regularly. And, true enough, Joy wouldn't be suffering so much from this issue if she had a stronger sense of herself and were less insecure. It's likely that neither one of them would be bothered as much by this issue if stress demands from Kevin's work weren't so high and both partners were paying more attention to each other. But that's not the way it is right now, so where can they go from here?

Any way we look at it, Sally is in the middle of their relationship. Perhaps Kevin can ultimately end up having friendly relations with her—sometime down the road when he has built a solid foundation in *this* marriage, with Joy. But right now there isn't enough time to do it all. He must make a choice— and a choice means sacrificing something. Does he want to be with Joy and get the most out of being with her? Or does he insist on keeping ties with his ex and sacrificing the best he can get out of his life with Joy (perhaps, finally, even sacrificing his life with Joy altogether if this goes too far). He has already discovered that hiding from the issue won't work.

If Kevin has no hidden attachments to Sally, cutting contact shouldn't be too difficult. He did, after all, participate in the end of their marriage. Of course, if he cuts contact, he will be worried about Sally's well-being, but the truth is that Sally is an adult and will get on in life in her own way, and maybe even a little faster if she's not so attached to him. (If she's not an adult, this will be her chance to find out and grow up!) If Kevin does have hidden attachments, some things might become clearer after he cuts off contact for a period of time. He might realize that he gets to experience himself as powerful when he's Sally's helper. He might see how his contact with her saves him from having to put both feet fully into his present marriage and thus keeps him from having to experience the vulnerability that comes when one commits wholeheartedly.

Pressure from All Sides

Their options seem clear; but this is real life, so there are a few complicating factors. One reason Kevin *cannot* cleanly cut his ties with Sally is that they have children. He also has alimony and support payments he must make to Sally and their children. And a year later, with the problem still unresolved, Kevin and Joy had their first baby.

Kevin, Joy, and their new baby are embarking on one of the great journeys of life: parenthood and deeper commitment to family life. Like all new parents, they are discovering that finding all the time and energy they need for themselves and their new family is a big challenge. In spite of his earlier hopes of putting in fewer hours at work, as a new father, Kevin now feels even greater pressure to make his new business a success. As he devotes more time and energy to his work, tensions on the home front are higher than they ought to be. In the middle of all this, Kevin is also attempting to be a good father to his children from his first family.

We see a lot of situations similar to the one Kevin and Joy are in. Joy wants to be understanding and wants to support Kevin's contact with his and Sally's children, but she feels that he should be attending more to his new family. Because she knows demanding too much is unreasonable, she has a tendency to mask her true feelings. But masking feelings does nothing to change them; they just build up underneath the surface (and lead to trouble later on).

In addition to the attention she loses to Sally and the Kevin-Sally children, the sensitive issue of money is present. Like all less-than-angelic (meaning: real-life) second spouses, Joy has come to resent the money that goes out of their household

toward alimony and child support. Intellectually, she is aware
that she was supposed to know what she was getting into in the
beginning—she *did* know—but that doesn't stop her from feeling resentment. She also stuffs these feelings.

Kevin, meanwhile, is overwhelmed. Trying to be a father and
provider for two families in addition to husband and career
person is taxing him to the limit. He feels guilty about the
breakup of his first family. He couldn't avoid seeing how
wounded his children were by it all, and he told himself he
would be the very best father he could be under the circumstances. That meant keeping up with the children's activities
and having regular input in major decisions. All that makes
regular contact with his ex-spouse a necessity. Joy's demands to
cut down on contact with Sally are hugely frustrating to him
because he couldn't do anything about that if he wanted to.

Rather than exposing his feelings about all this, when Kevin
gets even more pressure from Joy (direct or hidden) to cut back
on contact with Sally, he circles the wagons and closes off to
protect himself. Joy knew what she was marrying into and
should have been more prepared for the time he would need to
spend with Sally and the children. She should be more understanding and accepting. It all seems like too much. He just
wants Joy to lay off and stop adding to the pressure. Deep
down, he is feeling pretty angry about it all and frustrated that
he finds himself in a powerless position (he just can't do it all).

Even though Joy doesn't say much about it out loud, Kevin
knows she is annoyed that so much money goes out to his first
family. If he were to be truthful about it, that makes him angry,
too. He is angry about all the demands that are placed on him.
He is angry that he sees no "right" way to be with all this. He is
angry about not being appreciated for all he does and for his
considerable efforts to be a good father. He doesn't care to know
what he's feeling—he just wishes it would all get easier. So he
stuffs everything—and his way of stuffing is to withdraw even
further. Rather than talk more about these things, he says less.

As Kevin withdraws, Joy gets even less attention. Seeing herself as low in his priorities, she feels hurt and angry, but also

tends to stuff her feelings. Her baby is in the forefront for her, and she increasingly focuses on the baby for her sense of fulfillment. Before long, she finds herself feeling very nonsexual toward Kevin. She, too, withdraws and withholds. He has feelings about that, but stuffs these feelings, too. When so many stuffed feelings are around, couples get into a lot of little, picky arguments that always seem to go in circles. Both end up feeling dissatisfied, each wondering how the other could be so "thick."

We're not even talking much about the ex-partner or all the mixed (and stuffed) feelings over on that side. However: Sally is angry about being a single mother, about being financially dependent, and about a whole lot of other things. Part of her *would* like to sabotage Kevin's marriage with Joy.

Kevin and Joy are clearly in a very tight knot here. One is overwhelmed and the other is feeling starved. Neither of them is getting enough attention from the other. Loyalties are divided. Nerves are frayed. Both are sitting on a powder keg of feelings, but for the most part are stonewalling each other. Many players are involved, all with differing motives and needs. It would be oh-so-easy for them to throw up their hands at the complexity of it all or bury their heads and attempt to hide out. However, giving up will solve nothing, and just hoping for resolution *will not work*. So where do they begin?

Finding Resolution

Couples like Kevin and Joy are in a tough position, but they can find resolution *if they are willing to do what's required and go step by step*. First, they need more clarity about where they each stand. That will be greatly facilitated by their unstuffing some of their feelings, along the lines we have discussed in earlier chapters. After those feelings are expressed and received, seeing more clearly is always easier. (Remember, allowing *all* feelings—positive and negative—to flow leads to enhanced energy, more aliveness, and the ultimate emergence of positive feelings.) Next, each partner will need to locate and express his or her essential needs. Then comes the most important work of all: negotiating to get as many needs met as possible. After that, it is a matter of keeping up-to-date with agreements and following through rigorously. Let's go through it one step at a time.

Unstuffing Feelings

Partners in situations like Kevin and Joy's often spend too much effort trying to discover who is "right" and who is "wrong." Instead of cooperating to make their relationship all it can be, partners engage in verbal combat over the surface issue or compete to freeze the other out. As relations become more strained, they become hypersensitive to anything that sounds remotely like criticism and throw up defenses at a change of a voice tone or the raise of an eyebrow.

Expressing and receiving feelings at this stage, before the *real* rigidity sets in, is so important. As therapists, we wish we could leap into marriages at this stage and shake both partners. We would shout: "Get help now!" "Don't let too much time go by while you're in this state!" "Even though you are very busy, make your relationship a priority!" "It only gets tougher later on if you avoid feelings now!" "No one is right or wrong here— you both have strong feelings and you are both entitled to them." "If the territory is too charged for you to work it out yourselves, give therapists a try (and do it sooner rather than later, while it is relatively easy to repair!)" or "Don't waste your precious time together competing instead of cooperating!"

If Kevin and Joy don't bring out their stuffed feelings right now, they are setting the stage for the downward spiral of their marriage. For instance: We know that people who swallow their feelings eventually go numb. Joy, as a new mother with numbed feelings, buried resentments, and no way of getting them out, closes off to her husband. As she closes off to her husband, she becomes over-involved with her child—and even the child ends up suffering in the long run as a result of this unfortunate situation. Kevin, too, has to keep coming forward as opposed to retreating behind a wall as so many men tend to do. Only a man who is standing up, and fully present in his thoughts and feelings, can avoid being swallowed up by these two seemingly bottomless pits of demands from two women, from two families.

Getting to feelings and learning to express and receive them either takes a huge amount of determination and commitment to learn a new language or the willingness (especially in the beginning) to seek skilled professional help. We know that couples tend in general to resist seeking help, but the stakes are so high in situations like this that overcoming the resistance is well worth doing.

Fortunately, Kevin and Joy did seek help. With some of their primary feelings expressed, both calmed down considerably. Joy was relieved to hear that Kevin was angry about the pressure, payments, and responsibilities. As he came forward with his feelings (as opposed to his verbal justifications), she began to appreciate his position more. As Joy presented her feelings (as opposed to verbal assaults), Kevin began to receive some of her sense of urgency about developing a foundation for the new family. He really heard her experience of feeling left out and being low-priority. When honest feelings come out into the open, defenses come down.

Unstuffing feelings is a very important step. Partners need to get their inner experiences into the open in order to develop a more complete understanding of where they are with each other. When feelings have been received on each side, a greater willingness to negotiate emerges automatically. *Then* comes the necessity of finding a solution, which means discovering how to get the most important needs met. (Many couples attempt to directly meet the immediate needs, but this doesn't work nearly as well.)

Locating and Expressing Needs

It's too bad that locating and expressing deeper needs isn't easier—a lot of divorces could have been avoided if it were. Just like feelings, needs first have to be located, and that's a bigger challenge than most people realize. Then there is the problem of expressing needs in a way that can be understood and acted on. Partners must realize that, realistically, not all needs can be met in a relationship, but *unexpressed* needs are most likely to—are almost guaranteed to—go unfulfilled.

Joy realized clearly that she needed more attention. She needed to know that she is higher in Kevin's priorities than Sally, and she needed to be in on decisions he made about his children. Over the longer run, she also needed to know he will limit his all-out investment in his work.

Kevin needed more appreciation for all he is doing. He needed more rest from the tension on the home front. He needed some limits to Joy's demands on him about dealing with Sally, because he fears she will just keep on pressing for more than he can deliver. He had a difficult time saying it, but he needed more attention, too.

Getting these needs out in the open was not nearly as easy as simply writing them down in a list, as they are presented here. Most of us have just as much difficulty articulating our needs as we do our feelings. Somehow we are not supposed to be "needy," since needs often are associated with appearing to be weak or overly self-centered. In relationship, however, we all have needs, along (unfortunately) with a lot of magical expectations that our partners will fill them without our having to define them.

Once needs are out in the open, partners need to get to specifics (which is also more difficult than it sounds). They must ask themselves some basic questions. What would getting their needs met look like? What are they willing to give up in order to get their most important needs met? Rather than getting in wrangles about the ex-spouse, they need to ask themselves what they can do with *each other* to make things work better in their marriage. This leads to the work of establishing boundaries and agreements.

Establishing Boundaries and Agreements

The needs for attention or appreciation and freedom from conflict are very big, bottomless needs. Nobody is capable of completely meeting them. Clearly, some boundaries must be set. In order to do that, Joy and Kevin had to dig a little deeper.

Joy would like to have Kevin cut all contact with Sally and give her that time, but she can't have that. We pressed her to put some boundaries around her needs. In the short run, what bothered her most was being left out of the decisions that Kevin and Sally were regularly making—particularly those in regard to Kevin's children. When the children visited, she was called on to mother them and do motherly duties, yet she was being treated as an outsider.

She also resented not knowing when Kevin was making contact with Sally, and she wanted to be let in on that. In fact, every time he contacted Sally, she wanted to know. In this area of their lives, she didn't want any surprises. She knew this would probably be viewed by Kevin as over-controlling, but if he maintained these boundaries she would be a lot happier—regardless of how it looked.

Joy's needs are quite typical of spouses in second marriages. If contact must be maintained with the first wife, the second wife wants to be in on what's happening, and preferably be informed ahead of time. Most second husbands would also like to know about contacts between their wife and her first husband. It's not so much a matter of control as it is of courtesy. Like it or not, newer spouses often tend to be insecure in their position (after all, their partner did ditch the previous spouse), and this kind of arrangement helps to build trust. If partners find a way to get through the earlier phases successfully, these types of conflicts tend to fade away.

So far, Joy hadn't expressed anything Kevin couldn't agree to. Now we go to Kevin's needs. Kevin would like to have total freedom of action and total freedom from dissension over his contacts with Sally, but he can't have that. What bothered him the most were the frequent arguments about Sally that seemed to come up when he felt least equipped to deal with them. He needed more expressions of appreciation for all that he was doing. He also needed more cooperation around the alimony payments that went out each month.

As Kevin got a little clearer about what he needed, nothing emerged that Joy couldn't agree to in principle. But in precise terms, what was she supposed to do? Not ever talk about her feelings about Sally? That was impossible. Was she supposed to appreciate him every hour? Not likely to happen. Never again be disgruntled over alimony payments? Forget about it. In order to come to an agreement, partners need to work out specific terms, which means specific boundaries.

Here's a brief summary of what Kevin and Joy eventually worked out:

- Kevin wouldn't make contact with Sally without telling Joy; he would also discuss Sally's calls after they came. Kevin would consult with Joy on decisions regarding his children.
- If Joy had concerns about Sally she wanted to bring up, she would advise Kevin ahead of time and set up a specific, mutually agreed-upon time to discuss them, preferably over a weekend when there was more opportunity to do so.
- He would take the initiative and organize some special way of giving her attention at least once every two weeks.
- She would make a concerted effort to express her appreciation in a way that he could really hear it at least once every two weeks.
- As a couple they would set aside fifteen minutes a day, at least five days a week, to express what they had been feeling that day and what they were honestly feeling about each other at that moment.

These agreements can be summarized very succinctly: *He will move closer and she will back up.* None of the agreements require a terrible sacrifice. Both partners must give a little. Both will get more of what they need. Both will get a sense of strength by setting boundaries. In the give-and-take of the negotiation, both came to understand that in order to have the right to *set* boundaries in marriage, they must be willing to *receive* them. Both agreed to try out this agreement for three months to see what happens, then to renegotiate as necessary. In the meantime, they will have a period of peace and the opportunity to build more trust and vitality in their relationship.

This agreement is not the happy conclusion of all of their problems, but it is a start—a way of beginning a virtuous circle instead of adding to a vicious one. To some people, making agreements like these might seem clinical and unromantic. However, Kevin and Joy didn't feel that way at all. They were greatly relieved to know what was expected of them. Losses on both sides were more than compensated by gains. In fact, almost anything would have been better than the struggles they were having before.

Follow-Through

Follow-through makes or breaks a marriage. When both partners are still tender from a major struggle over a hot issue, a failure to fulfill the agreements is very damaging and trust is even harder to establish next time. Buttons are easily pushed in that area for quite a long time afterward. Until everyone's needs have been met for a meaningful period of time, emotional malnourishment will continue. Partners who are not nourished emotionally have a tendency to regress. *We cannot overstate the importance of follow-through, right to the letter.* Smashed boundaries and broken agreements provide the fuel for divorce.

Fortunately, issues with ex-spouses tend to calm down after the first couple of years. This period of tension will pass a lot more quickly if "attached" spouses remember a couple of things. Don't keep secrets about the ex: Be straightforward about everything concerning the ex. Even more important, remember that no matter how things look on the surface, the complaining partner needs *more* attention, not less. Even though it may feel like it is going against the grain sometimes, giving the new partner the attention he or she needs is the fastest way to get through the crisis.

9

Stepparenting: The World's Toughest Job

The bond between parent and child is one of life's strongest—stronger, one might argue, than the bond between the parent and new mate. How could it be any other way? The child is born of the parent; the child is an extension of the parent's self. This bond has been many years in the making, and every natural instinct favors its development. Complex needs have been met through this parent-child relationship over a number of years and then along comes this stranger: the new spouse.

Many people enter a second marriage unprepared for the monumental challenge of bringing children from the first marriage into the new relationship. Once the relationship between the stepparent-to-be and the child (or children) has passed the preliminary tests of compatibility, everyone assumes that all will be well after the marriage. Then, some time into the marriage, problems inevitably arise, and the new partners are ill-equipped to deal with them.

The challenges are clear: Rather than two people having to work things out, which can be difficult enough, three or more individuals must now come to terms with each other. (And when more than one child is involved, matters are even more complex.) Put three or more people together in the cauldron of life, at least one of whom has no real say in the matter, and you can be sure that many stressful scenarios are going to arise.

Rick and Patricia:
"I Know What's Best for My Daughter"

Rick and Patricia have been married for three years. Rick came into the marriage with a five-year-old daughter, April; Patricia, though married once before, had no children of her own. Rick and his first wife broke up early in their marriage, and Rick has had full custody of April since she was two. Part of the story is very familiar. Rick has been over-involved at work and not spending enough time at home. Patricia also works part-time and carries a lot of the family duties as well. There's not enough time, not enough attention, not enough feeling—and both partners have become depleted. In spite of a great beginning, they have begun taking each other for granted. In short, it's an ideal environment for hatching stepparenting problems (and just about every other kind of marital problem). Lately, Rick and Patricia have been disagreeing on how to handle a situation with Rick's daughter. Now eight, April is having difficulty sleeping through the night and calls out from her room most nights. Her dad goes over and sits in her room until she falls asleep. Rick feels as if his duty is to console his daughter, and he discourages Patricia from getting out of bed or even getting involved. At first, Patricia was pleased to see that her husband was such a devoted and caring father. Lately, however, she's been feeling resentful. She is being displaced as a mother, and her opinion is not being acknowledged. Patricia believes that April is old enough to get through the night without her dad coming in to sit with her each time she calls. Their nights get disrupted and April, Patricia is certain, is just playing for her father's attention. Rick counters that he has consulted his pediatrician, his guide in child-raising for many years, and been assured that April's behavior is a normal stage. He's been told by the doctor that he'd be better off not to worry too much about it. Patricia says she would like to go to April herself and try her way of dealing with it. Rick resists. They can't come to any agreement and the whole thing has turned into a major issue.

Rick is determined to hold onto his position; April is his daughter and he knows what is best for her. He also believes that Patricia has a tendency to be a little hard on April, which makes him cautious. Patricia believes she has a great relationship with April. She feels as if her insight is being discounted. Unlike Rick, she has been a daughter and knows some things he and the male pediatrician do not. Typically, Rick and Patricia tend to get lost in arguments over their respective philosophies of child-raising and lose sight of the deeper issues. As therapists, we try to bring them away from arguing about the "right" answer to this situation (which nobody really knows) to focus on what is really happening between the two of them.

We point out that Rick has not been devoting enough time to the family and, when he is around, his priorities seem to be based around his daughter. Maybe Patricia is jealous of his attention to his daughter. At first, Patricia denies this possibility; but as we work at it a bit, she comes around to admitting that she is a little jealous. In fact, she resents the considerable attention and affection Rick gives to April.

This is a typical sequence of responses. At first, stepparents don't want to admit openly that they feel left out of the affections between birth parent and child. They think that, as adults, they should be willing to sacrifice themselves and be above this kind of petty competition. The child is only a child, after all, and has needs that must be attended to. Stepparents should be bigger than such pettiness, above feelings of jealousy. They don't want to admit it, but that doesn't mean they don't have feelings about being prioritized second where attention is concerned.

What about Rick? He senses Patricia's jealousy, and he knows that he should be giving her more attention. But the demands of fathering are big enough by themselves, and he resents demands from his wife as well. In his opinion, she should be more mature and not so needy. He also resents having to defend April. Rick's response is typical of a birth parent. When there are conflicts over his child, he becomes guarded. He senses his partner's desire for more attention, but doesn't want to address that straight on. In his way of seeing things, his wife shouldn't even question his need to shower as much attention as possible on his child. He feels torn, and it seems to him it shouldn't be that way. He feels as though his being split like this must somehow be Patricia's fault for being too demanding.

If we want to look at this issue objectively, both partners are "right." The stepparent must be willing to accept second place at times, and the birth parent must become more inclusive. As things stand right now, however, both parents are missing this point. Rather than looking inward and seeing where each of them must develop as partners in a marriage, they are focusing all of their attention on April and the bedtime issue. But the roots of all of this go much deeper than April's night fears. Rick's actions strongly indicate he has given his heart to his daughter much more than he has given his heart to his second wife—and he can't see it. We'll explore the repercussions of this in more detail later in this chapter, but first let's develop a parallel consideration and look at Joe and Stephanie.

Joe and Stephanie: "Your Son Needs More Discipline"

When Joe and Stephanie met, Stephanie's son Chris was thirteen years old. Except for a couple of summers with his father, Chris has lived with Stephanie as a single parent for nine years. Now, two years into this second marriage, problems are arising—and Chris is not a small part of the issue. Now fifteen, Chris hasn't been doing all that well at school, and it's not because he isn't bright. Whatever the reason, he's not on any kind of focused or goal-oriented track in life and he's not hanging out with the kind of crowd Stephanie and Joe approve of or support. This much they agree on, but not much else.

Joe would like to see Chris getting a lot more discipline and structure. Chris seems to have a very low tolerance for frustration and, in Joe's view, part of the reason is that Chris has never been pressured to apply himself to any given task. Nor has he been held to completing tasks he has started. Chris further shies away from any situation that calls for overt competition, which is why Joe would like to see him in team sports, or at least in some activity that challenges him.

Stephanie doesn't believe that kids ought to have to engage in competition. She wants Chris to feel like a winner on his own terms, and she knows he is. She knows Chris is a good, talented kid, and she has every confidence that he will emerge intact and emotionally healthy from this stage he is now going through. As she sees it, Joe has a clear tendency to be hard on Chris. Joe's own father was hard on him, and frankly she doesn't think that approach has turned out to be so great for Joe. She sees Joe as a little stuck—certainly stuck in an outdated attitude toward child-raising.

The way Stephanie handles money with Chris is another hot issue for Joe. Chris should have to take responsibility for some chores around the house in return for the money he is given. If he wants to spend more than he receives, he should get part-time work and learn about earning money. Once again, Joe thinks Stephanie gives in too easily. Joe does his part, trying to hold the line with a defined allowance, and he feels undermined by the way Chris can almost always talk his mother into agreeing with his way of seeing things.

Stephanie admits she might give in a little too easily, but saying no is hard. Plus, it's not as if huge amounts of money are involved. She works hard, and part of the reason she does is so her son can have a few extras—extras she did not get from her own parents. She wants to do things differently than her own parents did. If she is prompted to be completely honest, Joe is not only too tight fiscally, he is also tight personally.

Like Rick and Patricia, Joe and Stephanie tend to find themselves arguing over "child issues" rather than going inward to feel their own feelings. Stephanie tends to focus on Joe as the problem and not face up to where her son is actually headed. Joe, too, focuses on Chris's direction (or lack of it), rather than exploring what is going on inside him (and the feelings he has as Stephanie aligns more with her son than with him). We therefore try to bring them both away from Chris and encourage them to look at what is going on between them, as a couple.

Joe reports that he sees Stephanie as too protective of Chris, much too soft; his masculine side is not developing as fully as it ought to be at this stage. Stephanie has a hard time hearing this—all she can see is that Joe is jealous of her affection for Chris and too hard on him as a result. She sees Chris as being at a formative stage and she doesn't want to alienate him by being too tough with him. She wishes Joe could be more accepting of Chris, more open to him.

After Joe and Stephanie have offered their "insights," we can still see that they are not going inside themselves. Joe doesn't want to admit to feelings of being left out; he doesn't want to acknowledge the feelings he experiences when his contribution is undermined. Stephanie still has most of her attention on Joe as the "problem" and is unwilling to look at what might be going on inside her. For example, birth parents often carry a lot of self-judgment about pain they have previously inflicted on their child by their participation in the breakdown of the original family. They feel like failures as parents. Rather than allowing these feelings to come through and working with them directly, they put up a shield and become hypersensitive about their child-rearing to the point of being defensive. They also tend to overcompensate with behaviors they secretly hope will make up for their child's deep disappointment. In this clouded atmosphere, permissiveness is confused with love and acceptance.

When partners refuse to look inside for the source of their difficulties, they almost always spend their time and energy attempting to pin responsibility for the problem on each other. Any objective observer can see that the whole family would make immediate progress by combining the best Joe has to offer with the best Stephanie has to offer. If they'd find a way to blend Joe's demand for boundaries, discipline, and accountability with Stephanie's recipe of acceptance, allowance, and support, they would end up with parenting and stepparenting techniques that have a chance of working. But if they continue using up their energy against each other, there isn't much hope for change in the family. In addition, this consideration looms: When parents have hidden conflicts, children have a tendency to feel these conflicts within themselves and then act out in ways that are disconcerting—it's a powerful reason for the parents to start getting these matters worked out between themselves without delay.

Ed and Rosemary

Before we go on to our analysis let's take a brief look at one more couple with stepparenting problems: Rosemary and Ed. Rosemary married early and had two children, divorced, and was a single mom for ten years. During those years she was always hoping to find the love of her life, a man who would also be a responsible and loving father for her children. Along came Ed, married once before, but without children. At first, he was the love of her life and seemed to get along fine with the kids. Rosemary was sure her prayers had been answered: A good man *and* a father who had come along just in time to help raise her teenage children. What more could she ask for in life?

However, she did not discuss her fantasy with Ed before they married. After the marriage, and for months later, she waited for Ed to step in and help parent the children. Instead she got the opposite of her wish—he seemed less involved as time went on. In fact, he left all the parenting to her.

Ed didn't disagree. On occasion he would relax and play with the kids, but when it came to the tougher demands like establishing boundaries or sacrificing personal time, he didn't see how or where he fit in—or even if he should. From his point of view, they were Rosemary's kids and he did not want to interfere.

As time went by Rosemary became increasingly disappointed and angry about Ed's reluctance to join the family and take on a full parenting role. She needed and wanted help and she told Ed so. Unfortunately, as her demands intensified, he retreated to the same degree. As he retreated her disappointment and anger became even more pronounced. A whole cycle of events began that put their marriage in jeopardy.

Let's see what's happening. Clearly Rosemary had unrealistic expectations. Although it would have been a great gift to find a man who jumped wholeheartedly, skillfully, and without reservation into the substitute father role, the truth was she picked a man who previously had no children of his own. He had no experience parenting and probably had fears about taking up that role. At best, Ed's progress would be slow.

At this moment the biggest problem is clearly with Ed. With a wife and two children to care for it would seem he is still trying to live like a single man inside a family. From Rosemary's perspective he seems to be in the role of another child instead of husband and father. Before hooking up with Rosemary he had been in his cave a long time, and that was a more comfortable place than the world of teenagers today. In order to move forward and take on the role of supportive husband and father, he has to feel his insecurity about parenting and follow through anyway. If he refuses to take his place as a father, he will continue to be treated like the son he has been playing out. This marriage probably won't endure.

What's Going On in
Stepparenting Families?

Every set of parents is going to have disagreements about child-raising. Every set of parents must work at finding ways to compromise for the betterment of the family as a whole. Stepparents face an obvious additional hurdle: The birth parent/child bond was already very well-developed before they came into the picture. The birth parent has already developed a set of mostly fixed views regarding how to bring up his or her child. The birth parent is also naturally protective, perhaps to the point of being defensive about the child's behavior. With that bond already strong between parent and child, the adult partners themselves are much more vulnerable to being divided. When parents are divided, they end up working against each other. If they end up working against each other, not only does their relationship suffer, but the child also doesn't get the best possible environment for healthy development and growth.

The Ideal:
A Strong Bond between Partners

In the healthiest families, the primary bond is between the parents. The strength of the parental bond provides an umbrella of protection and support over the family as a whole. In the best possible parenting environment, partners unite to combine the best of what each has to offer and they are willing to compromise with each other to ensure that the umbrella of protection is solidly supported. The child then gets a chance to develop in a balanced environment.

In order to create this ideal environment, each parent must also be able to acknowledge where he or she is a weak contributor, and then step back while the other offers strength in that area. Not "step back" as in abdicate, but as in allowing the other's wisdom when doing so seems appropriate. Clearly, finding this ideal is a lot easier to say than to do. Mistakes will be made. But if both parents are willing to keep bringing themselves forward and supporting each other in all of their decisions, a stable family environment will eventually emerge. If parents are willing to carry through with the disciplined work of strengthening the bond between them by bringing themselves fully into the marriage, hearing out each other's feelings, meeting each other's needs, surrendering to each other, and giving each other lots of time and attention, the chances are things will go well in the family. But that is not the way a stepparenting situation usually starts off.

The Real:
A Strong Bond between Parent and Child

In the first stages of a stepparenting marriage, the bond between birth parent and child is stronger than the spousal bond between parents. The tendency is for the birth parent to align with the blood child when conflicts arise—which means the tendency is for the marriage to go out of balance. Since the birth parent has lost a mate before (often under painful circumstances), the birth parent may be hesitant to trust the stepparent (or anyone!) with full parental responsibilities. After having spent many years bonded as a unit with the child, the birth parent will almost certainly have difficulty relinquishing control over what is *perceived to be* the child's best interest.

There are problems in this arrangement, problems the birth parent doesn't usually want to see. Underneath the surface of a strongly bonded parent-child relationship, the parent is often unconsciously looking for the child to fill intimacy needs, to fill a void of emptiness. Consciously, the parent is convinced that the child is the needy one, but really the parent has an even greater need for the child. As the parent looks to the child to fill their intimacy needs, distance from the spouse is created. As distance is created from the spouse, the birth parent *increasingly* relies on the child to fill those intimacy needs. Even more distance is then created from the spouse. If we follow this process along a few more steps, we see the prospects for long-term spousal intimacy starting to become clear. We can also see where the family as a unit is headed: to significant imbalance.

If the bond between birth parent and child is exceptionally strong, the chances are that no room is present for *any* stepparent to come into the scene. But if one does arrive, he or she soon becomes aware of the developing lack of balance in the marriage. This is a very touchy situation. On one hand, the bond between birth parent and child is a wonderful thing; on the other, if the bond is too strong, it doesn't leave enough room for the new mate. All of this is made more difficult because the birth parent doesn't see any conflict and has no real motivation to alter the special bond with the child. Add to this a multitude of other problems: lack of full trust that the stepparent will come through as a parent to the child; feelings of guilt about wounds created by the *last* split and a need to compensate for that pain; defensiveness about how the child was raised; the truth of how slowly real trust develops; a reluctance to let go of power and control. All this makes the birth parent highly resistant—or perhaps we should say "highly sensitive"—to any intrusion by the stepparent into the bond that has developed between birth parent and child.

These dynamics are usually not perceived consciously. But if we were to bring the hidden aspects out into the open, the stepparent who is committed to the job is, in fact, left with a major dilemma: Accept the status quo—which means accepting second place, accepting a marriage where the mate is more bonded to the child—and deal with all the consequences of that; or speak up and drag the mate (who is likely to be resistant) more genuinely into the marriage and attend to the work of strengthening the spousal bond. That means challenging a deeply entrenched system and risking the many powerful feelings that will inevitably arise until a new equilibrium is established—the equilibrium of two equal parents present with a child. This is a difficult situation. If the stepparent challenges the parent-child bond in any way, it can be seen as a self-centered intrusion. If the stepparent doesn't challenge the bond, it can ultimately lead to an untenable situation for the stepparent (and a dysfunctional family). A number of fine lines are also involved. At the beginning of a spousal relationship, the stepparent has little right to challenge the parent-child bond. A stepparent has to earn that right by proving that he or she is *capable of and committed to taking on a parental role over the long run.* However, if the parent-child bond goes unchallenged too long, no spousal relationship worth holding onto will remain. How can a relationship get to the "long run" in a way that is fulfilling and healthy for all parties?

The Way Through:
Transition to Trust

A successful outcome for this situation depends on realigning the bonds that exist in the family. Partners have to focus on strengthening the spousal bond and creating an environment where the child is parented by two loving adults who are fulfilled and in harmony with each other; where the parents are meeting each other's needs; where the parents don't have to look to the child to meet their own needs; and where the child is free to be a child. How do we get ourselves to that point?

Be Committed and Think Long-Range

The forces in this new family are very complex, and getting lost in them is almost too easy. When partners get lost, they end up feeling stuck and frustrated without quite knowing what is happening. Instead of coming together to work through the issues, they often end up polarized against each other, much as we saw in the case examples earlier in the chapter. The first step in dealing with this situation is to develop a guiding principle that identifies what needs to be accomplished. Establish early a mutually agreed-on intent that *partners will work on strengthening the bond between themselves.* In every conflict that comes up over children, partners must stop periodically, check inside, and ask themselves if they are, in fact, holding to this intent. That parents do this is also crucial for the children. Though their actions may not always show it, they need two parents *who meet each other's intimacy needs.* More than anything the parents say, what the parents do is what the children will be modeling as they develop their own styles of intimacy later in life. From what we have seen over the years, children who grow up overbonded with a spouse almost invariably end up having major difficulties with intimate relationships in their own adult years. During these early years that troublesome potential is not evident, but it becomes obvious later and is very painful to watch.

And one more thing: Following through on this intent will build a strong bond between the couple for the future. One day the children will be gone and they, the parents, will be left facing each other. If they have spent their energy aligning with their children and against each other, nothing will be left at that point. We wish we could offer a quick fix here, but the realignment of primary bonds—meaning strengthening the parent/parent bond and having that be the *primary* bond— is going to take years to accomplish. Along the way, will be many bumps, bruises, and slips, and maybe even a brawl or two. Parents must be in it for the long run and continually *prove* to each other that they are. This work is not for dabblers or for the "feint" of heart.

Locate, Share, and Receive Feelings

Once partners set a clear intent, they must keep on bringing up their feelings about all that is happening. As we have seen in earlier chapters, tracking feelings is the way through to truth and eventual clarity. Unfortunately, when stepparenting conflicts arise, both partners tend to hide from or simply ignore their feelings. The discontent then gets played out in the child issues—which is to say the child gets *used* because partners won't come clean with themselves, much less each other.

Birth parents often want to hide from the intensity of their need for their children. They want to hide from their feelings of anger when this bond is threatened. They want to hide from their feelings of resentment about being pulled in two different directions. They want to hide from their feelings of being parental failures. They want to hide from their fear that their mate might never care about their children as much as they do. They want to hide from their general tendencies to be defensive (and all of us defend when, deep down, we feel afraid of being seen for who we are).

Stepparents want to hide from their feelings of neediness. They want to hide from, or deny altogether, feelings that come out of being in second place in a loved one's eyes. They want to hide from any sense that they could be in competition with this much younger soul. They want to hide from feelings of resentment at being excluded. They want to hide from feelings of powerlessness when their insights and knowledge about child-rearing are not allowed to have importance or impact.

As partners hide from this multitude of feelings, everything gets tied up in surface issues and nothing real gets accomplished. The intent of forming a new and solid bond gets lost as partners end up using their energies against each other. As they run away from these feelings, they end up running away from each other, and the relationship can only go downhill. A lot of courage is required to locate, share, and receive difficult feelings, but the effort is worth it. If feelings are shared step-by-step along the way, the result is partners who stay connected with each other.

The Children's Role

We haven't talked much about the children's role in all this, and that's because the *parents* are the ones who need to work these things through. We should note, however, that the child gains a type of power when parents are using up their energies against each other. The birth parent usually has great difficulty attributing manipulative capacities to a sweet, innocent offspring. The stepparent, understandably, usually has less difficulty! Most children are not consciously trying to undermine the new spousal relationship; but, in the short run, doing so can work in the child's favor. This much is a given: Children want to continue to occupy the most special place in their parents' eyes, and anything that might get in the way of their doing so is a force children will confront. Further, divided parents are certainly much easier to overpower than those who present a united front.

Some parents believe in the myth that their children should assist them as they, the parents, seek to realign these bonds—a type of thinking that goes back to regarding the child as a source of succor. We repeat: *Changing these forces is not the task of the children.* Nor is making them easy a responsibility of the children. In fact, the children are almost certain to experience some discomfort as old bonds shift, for they will perceive themselves as losing power and influence; but they are just reacting to a pattern established by the parents. If the parents come through clear and true, the children will, in the majority of situations, adjust and be better for the experience.

We know that the experience of divorce and remarriage is tough on kids. In spite of any well-intended messages they get to the contrary, deep down they will assume responsibility for the demise of their parents' marriage, a fall from grace that came much too early. In spite of all the evidence that their parents are happy in their new lives (both parents might even be with new partners), their most heartfelt prayer for years afterward will usually be for reunification. Allowing a stepparent into their heart is tantamount to acknowledging that their dream of reunification is lost forever. It is a process that must go at its own pace and can't be forced.

Doug and Naomi:
Our Own Stepparenting Story

We have been through all we've written about here, and more. When we first became a couple, Naomi's two boys were in their teens. They were strongly bonded with their mother, which showed especially clearly in the way they were connected to her financially. Since their mother's breakup with their father, they had seen a couple of men pass through their lives with varying degrees of influence. When Doug came into the picture, they weren't all that excited about his presence. When we first lived together, Doug didn't get too involved in the discipline or the financial interactions, even though he had his doubts about some things. The fact is, when you have not married into the family, your input is limited. Until a partner has committed to really being there, he or she hasn't earned the right to have a controlling voice. It was safer to remain uninvolved. Once we were married, a few direct confrontations over child-rearing came into the open. Doug, for example, had different financial values than Naomi and her sons, and he began to demand more of a say in the way finances were handled. This, of course, was met with very strong opposing feelings. Naomi resisted Doug's increased involvement as much as the boys did. Rather than face these issues head-on, we would get into arguments over all manner of tangential topics—the same kinds of conflicts that came up in our case examples. Just because we're therapists doesn't mean we don't fall into the same traps as everyone else! Naomi's trump card was always the same: "You don't know my children like I do." She felt she had an even stronger position as the parent because Doug didn't have children of his own, and this was partially true. Doug had many things to learn. But Doug had experiences Naomi didn't have. Having been a teenage male himself, for example, he knew things she could never know. At times Naomi did know best, of course. But at other times she was blind to what was going on with her own children, and Doug's view was more objective.

At some point stepparents have to make a decision. Are they going to step up to the plate and take their position as a substitute parent with all that that entails? Clearly, that has to be the first move. Birth parents have to know the partner is committed to parenting before they can begin to let go. It took time, but Doug made that decision.

At some point, birth parents have to make a decision. Are they going to attempt to live in their marriage as single parents? Or are they going to *enter* the marriage and fully align with their spouse? Fully aligning means surrendering half the control of child-rearing, and this is a difficult task. On one hand, they welcome the support; but on the other, they really don't want much in the way of another person's interference with their view of what is right for their child (or children).

After a couple of years of marriage, it finally became clear that Naomi had to decide whether or not to allow Doug in as an equal parent. Part of that decision meant consulting him before making major commitments to her boys. In the beginning, it meant being careful even about minor ones. Naturally, that met with some initial resistance from her children. They didn't want these types of boundaries. But they had no choice other than to accept Doug's input. She had arrived at a clear decision and they understood that she was going to stand behind it, no matter what. Of course, her decision also required that Doug take a bigger step forward from his "observer" role and put forth more active energy as a father. This meant taking his lumps for some decisions that didn't work out for the best as well as experiencing the positive side of parenting more fully.

One other major turning point occurred when the boys were having some trouble with the stepparent on the other side— their birth father's new wife. Just like all kids who are uprooted from their families, their unconscious motive was to get rid of the new intruders and restore the old family. A meeting was called with all the major players. Both birth parents, in the presence of each other, told the boys in no uncertain terms that their marriage was over, never to be put back together. It was a statement of the obvious, but something major shifted after that day, when the announcement was made clearly and unequivocally. Even though the divorce was long past, the message had *not* been clearly stated before then, nor had it been received.

Twelve years later, the boys are grown up and we can safely say we've navigated the most difficult passages of the stepparenting minefield. But we've seen a lot of casualties in others' relationships along the way. For example, the most recent Joe-Stephanie type of pairing we've known didn't make it. The woman partner, unwilling to let go of control over her son, ended up choosing her son over her new spouse. A very sad outcome, in our opinion.

Focus on Your Relationship

The topic of stepparenting and blending families is very rich territory, and we do not have space here to address the myriad issues that arise: the interplay with the other birth parent; competition *versus* cooperation; dealing with inordinately hostile stepchildren; power and control struggles and conflicts over parenting styles that invariably emerge in blended families; stepsibling rivalry. We would also like to tie a nice ribbon around this topic and lay out six or seven foolproof steps for successful stepparenting—but, in our experience, that's not possible.

In the reality of stepparenting, there's some good news and some bad news. The bad news is there are no lasting solutions. The good news is there are no insurmountable problems. Partners who successfully cope are those who are determined to keep at it. Rather than succumbing to the temptation to hide from all the tender issues, partners must keep the relationship honest by staying up to date with each other about their feelings.

Partners must make every effort to create and to present a united front. In order to do that, birth parents must learn to pull back and stepparents must learn to come forward. We can only remind you once again of this central, supremely important fact: *Problems with the kids will almost always get sorted out eventually if the parents focus on keeping their own relationship honest, healthy, and loving.* Let the children be children and make every effort not to use them to play out conflicts that ought to be sorted out between the two of you.

10

<hr>

Yours, Mine, Ours: Money Issues

Mixing money with intimacy always creates challenges—and these challenges can become even more complicated in a second marriage. Some partners entering a second marriage worry more because they have more to lose. Some worry because they are getting on in life and believe they won't have enough to live on in later years. Not infrequently, complicated financial obligations to, or entitlements from, previous marriages add to the complexity.

Trust is often an issue. Previously married partners have witnessed at least one marital collapse. It is highly likely some of the most intense, painful, and possibly bitter aspects of the breakup occurred during negotiations over money. In these struggles, survival instincts and greed came right to the surface and stared each partner directly in the face. After these experiences, blind faith seldom remains fully intact.

Your Money? My Money?
Our Money

Our experience has shown us that a committed couple—partners who desire a relationship of two equally participating and evolving individuals—can't afford to keep their money separate. They must co-own significant assets and share mutual responsibility for all major spending decisions. How can they realistically and wholeheartedly each trust the other when they have no real history together? The short answer is: They work very hard at it!

We certainly weren't able to take this leap of faith right off in our own marriage. And, having witnessed many other relationships in our practice, we've discovered that many of the people who appeared to take this leap with ease at the beginning were simply hiding their true feelings. We'll discuss this more later.

It would be wonderful if we could lay out an unerring, universal road map to everlasting financial harmony in marriage, and especially in second marriages. Sure, we could present a series of general theoretical ideas like: "Believe deeply in abundance and everything will be all right." Or we could attempt to cover some specifics of budgets and balance sheets. But, in our experience, partners run into the worst money troubles when they won't openly communicate what is happening between them fiscally. They want to hide from the fact that a marriage is also a business between two partners who must actively engage in a lifelong process of negotiating equitable and hopefully prosperous experiences together.

In order to keep on top of this process, couples need to address their money issues—regularly and frankly. This means being willing to let go of masks and to bring out true feelings around money. Once thoughts and feelings have been expressed, partners need to develop agreements about money and be bold enough to challenge those agreements when they outlive their usefulness. It also means being wise enough to recognize that a stubbornly persistent money problem always indicates unexpressed feelings.

All this is easy enough to say, but it isn't easy to do. Couples tend to get stopped in the process, because almost everyone has a tendency to hide from feelings about money and to avoid talking openly about it. And so, before we get on to some case examples, let's look at this tendency.

Hiding from Feelings about Money

What's easier to learn about a couple: the state of their sex life or their annual income? As therapists, we usually hear a lot more about sex than income—unless we really press for specifics. Why is money so hard to talk about? In our culture, money is regarded as a way to quantify our personal power. Whether we like it or not, money is connected with how we are seen and valued by others—and how we see and value ourselves. It says a lot about how and where we fit into society.

Some people would prefer to believe they have risen above these mundane material matters, but folks who attempt to "rise above" money concerns also tend to be those who also have difficulty with intimate relating. A prosperous, juicy, intimate relationship that has staying power requires two individuals who are grounded and ready to deal with the realities of the life they live in—whether in regard to intimacy or money.

Money also smokes out the younger, underdeveloped places within partners. A woman who can cope perfectly well in the world on her own may revert to behaving like a daughter talking with (or hiding from) her daddy when money issues come up with her husband. A man may become defensive or unavailable—relating like a teenage son to his mother rather than a husband to his wife. We've seen partners who even refuse to turn up at personal budget meetings, fearing the need to be responsible or fearing being belittled by their partner. The hoarder, the addict, the dreamer, the frightened person, the boundaryless spender, and many more seldom-acknowledged internal characters all show through when money discussions are on the table in an intimate relationship.

Not surprisingly, people who are hiding from parts of themselves also hide from money conflicts. People don't want to see how childish they still can be. Neither partner wants to face the feelings of power and powerlessness that come up around money. Neither wants to stare control issues in the face or to experience the feelings related to being controlled. Partners don't want to acknowledge openly, and sometimes fight for, their own self-interest. The problem is this: Hiding of any kind in an intimate relationship can't work over the long run. Attempting to avoid money conflicts now only adds to difficulties later on.

Let's go now to some case examples and see what we can learn. In the first example, after eight years together in the current marriage, one partner is still attempting to maintain control of the assets. In the second example, one partner won't combine assets out of fear of losing them to the other's heirs. The third story is about us, for we as a couple had both of these challenges and others as well! In our own example, we'll talk about the process we went through and outline some specifics about how couples can navigate a few of the trickier fiscal passages.

Mick and Lisa:
Separate Bank Accounts

Mick has been married twice before, Lisa once. They've been together eight years. She came to the marriage with very little money; he had lots. Like many new partners in the romantic glow, neither talked much about how they were going to deal with this disparity before they got married. Lisa brings in a good income but still doesn't make anywhere close to the money Mick does in his job. Over the years, Mick has been adding to a substantial investment portfolio, which he proclaims is "theirs" but which he keeps in his name. They rent the house they live in.

When they first came into our office, both had very hard looks on their faces. We could guess they hadn't had sex in quite a long time, and maybe their situation was a lot worse than that! After the formalities, Lisa said she had reached the point where she wanted them to be in a home of their own. She was middle-aged now and needed to put down roots. She wanted, for instance, to be able to decorate with the long-term picture in mind, to have an environment that reflected something about her. She had told Mick and he had agreed to the idea—in principle.

She explained that they started doing the practical work by checking into the local real estate market. Prices were on the high side and they couldn't find a house that was mutually acceptable. Then they began focusing on raw land, with the idea of building their own house. This search had been going on for just short of a year. No matter what direction they turned, some hurdle always seemed to come their way. Both were experiencing high levels of frustration, and both were discovering that unresolved money issues had a way of bleeding over into other areas of life. (Indeed, their sex life was suffering.)

As we listen to Mick and Lisa, we know that this couple has the means to begin this important financial project but cannot carry through on it. We know it is not due to a shortage of land or houses. We hear both partners speaking in favor of the project. We also hear some hesitation to talk about money and we see disparities over financial control. There must be feelings going on underneath all this that are not being expressed. So we begin by encouraging them to bring things more out in the open. Why haven't they moved on this house dream?

As an opener, Mick says he believes Lisa was unrealistic about what they could afford. The only houses she clearly shows excitement about are thousands of dollars beyond what he would like to spend. Lisa says that's not true. She is willing to adjust her sights if he will just get definite about making a choice—he is so afraid of making the wrong decision that he won't make any at all.

Now we are seeing that both partners are totally outside of themselves, focusing on the other (the state of affairs, as we have already seen many times, that is almost always present when partners find themselves in a knot). As a way of getting closer to the root of the difficulties, we attempt to bring them back to basics: How much can they afford, and where is the money coming from? Both partners begin to shift uncomfortably, so we know we are heading in the right direction.

The One with More Money
Has the Power

As the story unfolds, we learn that Lisa still doesn't have much savings of her own. Mick must make the final decision about the house because it is "his" money. With "her" paychecks she covers half the household expenses, buys her clothes, and generally looks after her needs. Mick pays the other half of the expenses, pays for his needs, and has money left over to add to "their" portfolio. He is, she explains, rather secretive about it, but hints that its value is equal to about four houses in the price range they are looking at. They could (he says hesitantly) use the investment money to buy the house, but he needs to study the tax consequences (along with this and that, one thing and another). Clearly, he has difficulty letting go of control of the money.

Now the picture is getting clearer. What are Lisa's feelings about all this? At first, Lisa says she is feeling frustrated. As she begins to allow her true feelings out a little more, she gets to anger. Underneath her pride at holding her own financially, she says that she has always hated struggling to keep up financially. She resents the way he keeps the money in his name—to her, it signals a lack of trust.

Mick is pretty surprised at Lisa's strong feelings. He doesn't see himself as having control. In fact, he sees himself as a generous man. As he put it, he has "never denied" Lisa anything she really wanted. He wants a house for the two of them; it's just that so many factors are in the mix that he hasn't been able to get clear on which way to go. He loves Lisa and wants their marriage to work.

Let's stop and look at what we have so far. It's pretty clear: Mick is holding control. He says the investments are for both of them; but since he keeps them in his name, his actions speak much louder than his words. As he resists transferring "his" money into an asset that would be in joint title, he is saying, in effect, that he has no intention of letting go of that control. Yet, surprisingly, he is not fully conscious of what he is doing. (We see this quite a bit. Even though what's happening is obvious to anyone looking in from the outside, the one who is holding power and control doesn't quite see what's really going on. But the other partner always gets the message—and there is always a consequence.)

It's fairly easy to see where Mick and Lisa are heading. Money is a symbol of power, one of the biggest such symbols in our culture. Mick is withholding his power from the relationship—which really means he has withheld himself. As he has withheld himself, Lisa has been getting angrier and more resentful. Not only that, but his holding onto the money has automatically left her in a powerless, childlike position (which it would do with anyone). That creates another whole round of feelings in Lisa, all of which are related to being less than equal; and being less than an equal partner in a marriage isn't fun. Nor does it stop there.

The One with Less Money
Feels Undervalued

As Lisa continues to make less money than a partner who keeps his own earnings in his name, she begins to feel resentful. Her contribution is undervalued. She may not bring in as much money, but she brings many good qualities to the relationship that can't be quantified: her humor, her caring, her sensuality, her capacity to listen, and much more. Further, she cooks more than he does, gets groceries, cares for the house— all that, and she pays for half of the expenses by doing a job she works just as hard at.

Let's step back again and look at this situation. Mick keeps control of the money and Lisa is left in a powerless position relative to him with regard to money. Mick doesn't see any problem here because he is holding the power—at least up to the point when they buy the house; in his eyes things are just fine! Not only is Lisa feeling powerless in the money realm, she is feeling undervalued for the genuine contribution she makes to the marriage. After all, she shares all of what she has (both what she has on the inside and what she makes on the outside) while he doesn't.

When a partner feels powerless and undervalued in a marriage, you can bet that a lot of very strong feelings are present somewhere. In large part, Lisa has been hiding from these feelings in herself; and as she has hidden from her feelings, she has become closed emotionally and then sexually. This sequence is almost inevitable. When one partner withholds money, the other begins to withhold something of importance as well. Quite often that "something" is full sexual presence. Usually it isn't done with conscious intent, since loss of sexuality for the withholder of sex obviously hurts that person, too—but still, it's done.

We're beginning to see here that power imbalances over money have a strong tendency to create an unfortunate byproduct—sexual deadening. It usually happens gradually. First intercourse becomes less frequent. Orgasm becomes elusive. It starts with one partner, then sooner or later the other deadens, and the net result is that *both* find themselves in a sexually dry relationship without quite knowing how it all happened. Sad, but this is often a consequence when financial power is not fully shared.

In the end Mick might discover he values financial control more than a rewarding, fully participatory sex life with Lisa. Don't laugh. It would appear many older folks find themselves in that position when they get to the truth of it. The short-term way around that problem is to seek a much younger partner who might, *for a time*, accept the position of his minority shareholder. But, right now that is not the way he is thinking.

Trust Issues

Now let's get back to the matter of unexpressed feelings—this time, Mick's. They didn't always divide up expenses like roommates. A couple of years ago, he just got tired of trying to reconcile the checks in a joint account. Lisa didn't make any real effort to keep the checkbook balanced and she did a poor job of maintaining records. He also discovered the extent to which she had overspent on their credit cards. They got into so many fights about the way she handled money that he just gave up. By dividing up the expenses and keeping separate accounts, they got into fewer fights.

Furthermore, even though the investments are substantial, he fears not having enough to carry them through their retirement days in the style of living to which they have become accustomed. He is well into his fifties now and likely won't be making the same money he does now for too many more years. He had seen the way Lisa was capable of spending, and it scared him. She hasn't ever really indicated that she is concerned about their long-term financial picture, which leaves him carrying the responsibility. In fact, he felt some anger about all this. But rather than getting his deeper feelings out in the open, he retreated—quietly, without revealing what was actually happening inside himself. Separate accounting seemed like the only answer, certainly easier than pulling up and dealing with his true feelings.

Lisa says Mick is out of date. She admits overspending in the past, but she has changed. As she reflects on it now, part of her was very angry back then, too—and for basically the same reasons she is now. Blowing the budget was her way of getting back at Mick for his control over money, for the way he held power over her. Back then, just like today, she felt hurt and unappreciated for all the nonfinancial contributions she made that he didn't recognize. Getting nice things for herself was a way of feeling better. She acknowledged that her excesses stemmed from an immature part of herself, and she had resolved long ago not to let that happen again. But by refusing to let her forget it, Mick was conveniently using her past actions as an excuse for holding onto control.

As objective observers, we can see that Lisa is taking responsibility, but we're also hearing some victim statements. She did what she did, but a lot of what she did "was because of him and what he did." (In other words, he was to blame for what she did.) We can reliably predict that Mick will pick up on some of this, become defensive, and need to find even more ways she was at fault—and around and around the blaming circle we go. If this pace keeps up, at least another year will pass before their dream house becomes a reality—if it ever does.

It's true. When money is out of control, as it was for Lisa at that earlier time, the child inside is certain to be active. But that was a couple of years ago and it hasn't occurred since. So one must ask: At what point must Mick let go of the past and trust what is going on now? What would it take for him to trust her? Is he even capable of trusting—or will he just have to go on attempting to control everything himself? The chances are she would have a valid claim on the money if she went to court. What will it take for her to prove it? A divorce?

In summary, this relationship is stuck. Mick has been holding financial power by keeping the assets in his name. He keeps another, more subtle form of power by holding the perspective in his mind that Lisa is not entirely trustworthy. Lisa, however, is making it ever clearer to him that a partner cannot hold power in one area of relationship without suffering a consequence in another. Something significant in the way they handle their financial situation must change if they are going to become unstuck.

This house project has not come to fruition because they both have been hiding their feelings. No one knows what the outcome will look like, but they do need to get started on a process of exploration. Both have to come out with what they are feeling inside about the way money is handled in their marriage, speak up about needs, and get clear. In order for some growth to occur here, both partners have to become more honest about themselves.

Mick has to become more conscious of the way he holds power and control. He must adjust his view of himself somewhat, from the image of himself he would like to hold (prudent but generous) to recognizing what's true (he's a hoarder of control). Then he must look at what is underneath that. He needs to discover and disclose more about his financial fears. Sharing the money might feel to him like a loss of self (in which case, what kind of self does he really have?). He needs to acknowledge the anger and disappointment he has experienced over the way Lisa has handled money. He has to talk about what would be required in terms of specific behaviors if he is to loosen up control.

Lisa, in turn, has to share more about the anger and sense of powerlessness she has felt relative to his control in financial matters. She must look at her disappointment at having such a control-hungry partner. She has to recognize she has been something of a child, because here she is in her fifties, without the means to buy a house—and that is not an adult position. She has put herself in a position where she still needs "daddy" to get what she wants. She needs to look at how powerless and unassertive she is in regard to men, and how she has, for much too long, been avoiding confronting Mick over the way he has continued to stockpile assets in his name. She must realize he is unlikely to change without a push from her.

Where Can They Go from Here?

Together, they need to air out grudges from the past and develop a plan about how they are going to proceed. What are they going to do about that investment portfolio? How can they arrive at a more equitable agreement on sharing income? With some of this out in the open, and presumably an agreement to proceed with the house, both must begin talking seriously about how much is to be spent, where priorities are, and where sacrifices will be made. Then come the pragmatic decisions about tax consequences, borrowing, monthly costs, and so on. All of this is going to require give-and-take on both sides; but if both parties stay in the ring—with honesty—some kind of solution will eventually emerge.

If Mick and Lisa are not willing to get at their true feelings about money now, we can assure them that, based on our observations, lawyers and divorce courts will work wonders at helping them come out with their true feelings about money later! (And then their divorce lawyers can go out and buy houses with their fees.)

As it is, Mick and Lisa have been choosing to avoid all of this by keeping their accounts separate. Keeping separate accounts helps to avoid "money emotions" for a time; but in a marriage that is supposed to have two equal partners, it is more like a head-in-the sand approach. "Let's keep our money separate and that way we can pretend there are no money issues between us." But that really means: Let's not face the problem so we can pretend there is no problem. The trouble is, money issues are fundamentally important to any marriage, and they won't go away just because they are ignored.

Jim and Marcy:
"My Money Is for My Son"

Jim and Marcy are also a middle-aged couple, both in their second marriage. They have been married just over a year. Their sex is juicy. Both make about the same amount of money and both are willing to fully pool what they make. They share a house and operate within a mutually agreed-on budget. Day-to-day, financially, they do just fine.

To understand their problem, we have to go back to the days of their courtship, which was quite a long one. When they came together, Jim had more assets than Marcy. He was by nature a generous man and since Marcy had some money of her own, money itself didn't seem like a major issue. The issue was Jim's reluctance to get married.

He fudged around a long time, but finally it came out. Marriage, he acknowledged, meant pooling their assets. Marcy had four grown children, none of whom he felt particularly close to. He had one son. Having had sole custody, he felt very close to this son and, of course, wanted the very best for him. He wanted to marry Marcy, but knew it would mean adding four new potential heirs to his money. With Marcy, he was happy to share his money—but what if he died first? His son would get only a one-fifth share of the total estate and, who could know, maybe not even that. (Strange things can happen if families decide to fight over inheritances.)

Marcy felt hurt. After all, her children were an extension of her. A rejection of her children by Jim was akin to a rejection of her. She felt wounded by his stance. He was sorry she felt wounded, but he would not budge.

The urge to marry eventually overrode this issue, but before it did, a few more years of their courtship passed. During that time, Marcy didn't talk about the matter much, though she did continue to feel as if she was second in priority to Jim's son. But because she wanted to get married, she pushed those feelings away, though deep down she still felt hurt and angry about it. Jim also still felt angry that she should even question his desire to support his son as he saw fit. If she had wanted her children to have more, she ought to have taken responsibility to set that up during the earlier part of her life. He (and thus his son) shouldn't be penalized for doing it the way he did it.

Because so many tender feelings emerged the few times the topic was broached, the underlying issue had never been met head-on. As a result, it still lay beneath the surface, like a semi-tranquilized alligator. Thus Jim's assets (including the house they lived in) remained in his name, and neither partner talked much about the situation.

This kind of financial conundrum appears all the time in second marriages and, once again, there is no single, right solution to it. On the one hand, Jim's concern for his son's security is noble, arising out of a near-primal instinct to care for one's children. On the other hand, his commitment to Marcy is a commitment to bring all of himself to her and to have an allegiance to her. Jim would like to believe he can have it both ways—allegiance to Marcy and allegiance to his son. In Marcy's view, however, actions speak louder than words. So long as Jim keeps things the way they are, his primary allegiance is demonstrably to his son.

Whatever the eventual outcome of this situation may be, some kind of price will have to be paid. If Jim fully commits to Marcy (that is, commits his money as well as his heart) he is going to sacrifice some control of his assets. If he holds onto full control, he is essentially choosing to support his son's financial security over committing fully to her. We've already seen that when one partner withholds full commitment, the other will eventually pull back a piece of himself or herself, as well. When Jim withholds full financial commitment, Marcy is eventually going to withhold her fullest emotional commitment. Withholding leads to withholding leads to distance leads to protection leads to coolness leads to undernourishment leads to less-than-fully-alive partners.

Maybe some kind of middle ground can be found that will be satisfying to both, but that can't happen when partners avoid honest talk about the issue. As it is right now, both are attempting to avoid paying any price by not talking about it. We predict that it won't work over the long run. Even though the partners may choose not to talk about it, both are watching each other carefully.

Couples who avoid dealing with money problems directly inevitably find themselves in circumstances where the feelings bleed through into other areas of their lives. And as we saw in our earlier example, one frequent consequence is sexual diminishment. So far that hasn't happened to Jim and Marcy, but we would suggest they stay alert to the possibility.

Doug and Naomi:
Our Own Money Story

Fighting over money issues was not the only thorn in our early years together, but it was the biggest one. Anyone who'd seen us in those days would have had a good laugh when they found out we were couples therapists. In working with our own issues around money, however, we learned quite a bit that we'd like to share with you now.

Our situation was tightwad (Doug) meets one who likes to spend (Naomi), a pairing that seems to happen a lot in intimate relating. The one who likes to hold onto money is, for some strange reason, attracted to a partner who likes to spend (not so strange really, as it gives both partners a great opportunity to grow and develop new parts of themselves!). Making money comes easy for Naomi and she usually has a relaxed attitude about it. Rattling around Doug's psyche were remnants of Depression-era thinking passed along by his father. He is interested in detail, more focused on keeping track of money and minimizing expenses than he is at actually making money. All in all, it makes for an interesting match and presents great possibilities for attaining ultimate balance—but only if the partners find ways to combine strengths instead of competing. And that doesn't happen until a thorough discussion has taken place over money issues.

In addition to our innate differences, Naomi entered our relationship with significantly more money than Doug. The partner who has more money usually seems to have more control, and Doug didn't want her to have it. She didn't see the problem in the big terms he did, since—after all—she had the money! As the glow of the romantic stage softened a little, we ended up power-struggling over other issues, but our conflicts always seemed to find their way back to money. Neither of us was happy about this development, and several times our relationship was stretched to the limit of our mutual tolerance.

Fortunately, we had made an early commitment to be truthful with each other. Even in the middle of one of these conflicts, most of the time we were able to hold onto that inner observer who could see that we were getting closer to the truth. A conflict that is leading partners closer to truth can be exciting—and it *was* exciting! Instead of abandoning each other, we kept coming up against each other, and slowly we began to discover that our control issues had deeper roots. This meant that if we were to get anywhere with our money issues, we needed to come to terms with what was happening beneath the surface.

Searching underneath the conflicts over dollars, we eventually became aware that a very frightened and angry young person was living inside each of us, and that person had major fears about being financially powerless. Though both of us abhorred showing neediness (even to ourselves), deep down, the truth was that *each of us was needy* and had a wish to be taken care of by the other. We discovered internal aspects of ourselves who would be willing to sacrifice love for security. These internal "children" were very afraid of being abandoned or used. We also discovered *other* children, egocentric ones, who wanted every bit of the money and power for themselves! These various characters were covered over by masks of our preferred self-images, those of confident, secure adults.

Discovering these children inside each of us was obviously not an ego-enhancing process, but it helped us make a lot more sense of the knots we sometimes found ourselves tied in. Further, when we were able to direct our search inward, we discovered that the outer problems diminished in stature. When feelings were finally out, expressed and received, the resolution of an issue would almost always appear a short time later. Slowly the solution became clear: When money conflicts arose, we either had to do this kind of internal work or spend our energies tangling with each other over money and getting nowhere fast.

We also discovered that when we struggled with each other over power or control, our financial well-being as a couple suffered almost immediately. For example, when we are working together in harmony, our business phone rings all day long. When we are out of harmony with each other or struggling over power and control, it stops ringing. Most couples don't get the opportunity to see in such a direct way how powerful this correlation is, but we did. As a result, we have come to believe that partners' financial well-being has direct linkages to their emotional well-being as a couple.

Merge Assets Sensibly

For two people to merge all of their assets with reckless abandon would lead to as many difficulties as holding everything separately. So the question we were up against was this: How could we merge assets in a sensible way, in a way that corresponded to the growth of trust?

Clearly, the merge won't—and probably shouldn't—happen overnight. From what we have seen, the first three years of any marriage are a major testing phase, for combining finances as well as for almost everything else. Then, if you work hard at building trust for the next three to four years after that, you ought to be getting there. If not, serious questions deserve to be asked.

Open a Joint Checking Account We needed to develop a strategy that would help us to build this kind of foundation. The very first step was opening a joint checking account and paying for living expenditures out of that account. That may sound like an obvious thing to do, but we have seen a surprising number of couples who won't even merge an account to cover joint expenses. We believe it is an important first step.

When they're operating from the same account, partners have to face each other financially. Who puts in what? Equal amounts or some proportion according to income? What are the expenses as a couple and as individuals? Does working together on this come easily or are there constant struggles? Can a sensible budget be sustained over the long haul? Each partner gets a good opportunity to look at the other's sense of fiscal responsibility. We jumped this hurdle without too much difficulty.

Live within a Budget Next comes learning to live within a budget. As partners learn to stick to a budget, other important issues get smoked out. Limits have to be faced head-on. Power struggles often emerge over the way money is spent. If you can't work through a budget, you probably can't work through personal power struggles. And if you can't work through personal power struggles, you'll have great difficulty finding power as a couple.

Moving Slowly

As noted earlier, Doug had some money of his own but Naomi had considerably more. Having access to more money, she had more power, certainly more power to make decisions. For example, she could decide to get something special for the house, while Doug could only observe or comment. That went okay for a year or so, but eventually he discovered resentment building. One day Doug asked Naomi to consider separating out whatever she wasn't willing to share with him into a pot, separate from them. That pot, he suggested, would be in her name but not accessible to her on a day-by-day basis.

That led to some interesting discoveries. At first she agreed, but later discovered she didn't really want to be separated from her money in that way. Poking at Doug's fears around money was much more fun. However, the prospect of putting some of her money away, beyond her everyday reach, compelled her to examine more closely the way money gave her a built-in sense of safety and security in the world.

She decided to go along with his plan. This financial strategy helped in a number of ways. What we had together and earned together, we shared equally, which led to a feeling of sharing power equally. It also forced us to live a lifestyle that we had to develop for ourselves, rather than either of us depending on old money for bolstering or support. But it didn't force her to give up the ultimate security of having her money or push her into trust she wasn't ready to feel.

It looks to be easy for the one who has less money to suggest sharing it (actually it isn't!). But one thing is for sure: the decision to share one's money unconditionally is not an easy step. Rushing into it just so the other partner doesn't have to experience powerlessness is not a great idea either. That system took a while for us to work out, but when we did, it worked well—for a time.

After about three years together (we were married by now), we saw a new house that would work very well for us. Unfortunately, it was out of our price range at that time and if we wanted it, Naomi would need to take a draw from her own fund. She was willing to do that, but wanted a higher percentage of ownership of the house. Doug, however, wouldn't agree to going into our primary house as less than a half-owner. After a lot of wrangling, he agreed to sign a note for the extra amount she brought in.

Once again, this process is easily summarized, but that agreement required a lot of prior give-and-take. Each of us had to weigh in with our values, beliefs, and trust levels, and that agreement resulted in our having financial peace for a long time. (In the end, we made a very good return from that house and some years later Naomi tore up the note.)

About seven years into our marriage, we were still keeping her "old" money separate. She had a strong desire to bequeath her assets to her sons, the assets she had accumulated before we met. We went through a lot of ups and downs about the mechanics of how to go about doing that, but eventually we set up a trust in Naomi's name, the beneficiaries of which were her sons. We borrowed some from assets we held in common in order to allow her to create a trust about equal in value to the capital she had when we met. With the trust in place as a separate entity, that left everything between us totally under mutual ownership (with the exception of rather small accounts we kept separately for personal discretionary expenditures). This arrangement has worked smoothly for a number of years now, but it's probably not the end of financial friction.

A Lifelong Process

Working through money issues in a marriage is a lifelong process. (And if you believe you don't have any money issues, we suggest you look a little deeper—you may be fooling yourself.) If our experience has general validity, we can say now that the earliest struggles were hardest. Once we developed a spirit of cooperation and trust levels were higher, talking openly and negotiating became easier. But it's not over. We'll always have to work at forming agreements around those expenditures that each of us desires to make separately from the other. We need to work on savings plans and decide on the compromises we must make in order to build on them. One day we'll need to deal with inheritance money, another issue that many partners in second marriages struggle over. Any time a conflict comes up, we'll probably need to start right in again—expressing to each other what we believe in, risking exposing impolite levels of self-interest, and listening hard to the other's views.

The child within us believes that smooth money management ought to come easily, and that child would prefer to avoid facing these types of issues directly. In truth, it takes a lot of effort, negotiation, and creativity to find a balanced way of dealing with money in a second marriage. Both individuals need to get honest about where they stand with it. Both must be willing to locate, express, and receive the myriad of feelings that come up around money issues. Both partners must realize that *avoiding* won't work. When underlying feelings and power differentials caused by money conflicts are not addressed and avoidance has been the partners' strategy for dealing with them, repercussions are inevitable—repercussions that often are ultimately more painful than whatever problems would have emerged from dealing with the matters cleanly and directly, early in the relationship.

A nourishing and lasting relationship means working through money concerns *thoroughly*. When every bit of the money is not under total joint control (and how often is that?), significant and perhaps difficult feelings are going to be evoked. That's a given. Instead of holding back and building resentment, take a deep breath and summon the courage to face the issues that arise head on. Then, together, confront it and slowly unravel it, step-by-step, with one ultimate goal: equal partnership.

11

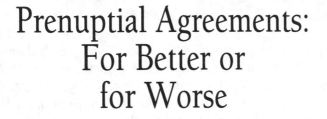

Prenuptial Agreements:
For Better or
for Worse

A second marriage often means two partners with unequal personal assets and complicated obligations left over from previous marriages. Successfully combining assets, as we have seen, is crucial to commitment. Yet many couples jump into a commitment without full consideration of how they are going to deal with their money—and it's no wonder, because financial issues are very emotional business. And drawing up a prenuptial agreement can be the most emotional business of all.

In the end, whether to have a prenuptial agreement must take into account what works for the couple in question. The most important action for partners to take is to talk openly about assets and make clear decisions about how to deal with them. It is very easy to say that insisting on a prenuptial agreement is like coming in with your bags packed, consciously or unconsciously preparing for an exit, but it's not so easy if you are the one with the money! So let's dive in and explore the territory.

What Is a Prenuptial Agreement?

A prenuptial agreement is a legal contract used to define control of assets. It is frequently called for when one partner is bringing significantly more assets into the marriage than the other. The primary aim is to protect those assets from being claimed by the partner at a later date. Clearly, boundaries established early make for less conflict later on. Even though consciously tackling a "pre-nup" up front can be very stressful, after it has been successfully negotiated, feelings of relief are often present all around—particularly if the process was thorough and both parties were honest about their feelings.

As we saw in the last chapter, money is a form of power. As one partner controls more assets, he or she always has more power and control in the relationship. In ordinary circumstances a couple grows together with the intent of forming a whole, a unit with two equal individuals operating together. Prenuptial agreements have a tendency to perpetuate imbalances and inequities. With a pre-nup in place, partners have no incentive to work on building the trust that it takes to create that unit. Over a period of years, the partner with fewer assets begins to feel as if he or she is committing everything, whereas the holder of the agreement is not. When one partner is under continual control of the other in any area of relationship, and when the controlled partner feels as if he or she is putting more into the relationship than the other, deep resentment is sure to follow.

Here's the dilemma: Putting together a prenuptial agreement is a common-sense, mature act that takes into consideration the realities of the modern-day world of intimate relationship. Yet it is also a document based on a lack of trust, and it puts into place a built-in power disparity that will affect the relationship in significant ways for years to come. Unless the partner with fewer assets is numb, completely under the spell of romantic love, or overawed by a partner with deep pockets who can afford to provide him or her with a lifetime of security, signing away specific personal rights to an intimate partner's assets is a highly charged experience—as we shall see in the following case example.

Anne and Hal:
Negotiating a Pre-Nup

Hal and Anne are in the process of negotiating a prenuptial agreement. Anne is coming into the relationship with significantly more assets than Hal and feels an agreement is necessary before she commits to marriage.

They had been together about a year when Hal proposed marriage. Several weeks after saying yes, Anne mustered the courage to mention that she would like to draw up a prenuptial agreement. The situation she was going into seemed all too familiar. Her ex-husband also had significantly fewer assets. She hadn't pushed for a prenuptial agreement, and ended up feeling fleeced by the divorce settlement. Hal already knew that she felt badly abused, and was hurt and angered by that experience. She believed that since Hal clearly loved her, he would understand her needs in regard to her money. She felt he would strive to ease her fears and know that, this time, she needed to get more clear about financial matters in advance.

When Hal heard her request, his immediate reaction was to cooperate. He wanted to demonstrate (to her and all others) that he didn't want her for her money. He wanted to distinguish himself from her previous husband, the "bad guy." He knew Anne still carried wounds from that involvement and he wanted to contribute to her healing, to do his best to assure her that he was totally present for her.

After a few days, however, the implications of signing a life-long, legally binding relationship agreement began to sink in. He started thinking that, fundamentally, Anne did not trust him. Here he was, committing all of himself and all he had, while his partner was not committing all of *herself*. Her entry into the marriage was conditional, his was unconditional. That left him at a disadvantage, as a less-than-full citizen in his own marriage. He should, he felt, be trusted as the honorable person he was; it should be obvious that he would never abuse this woman he loved so much. Unfortunately, he held these thoughts back until they were in the lawyer's office discussing the contract.

The lawyer's long list of questions highlighted the areas of conflict. Though negotiations appeared amiable on the surface, Hal felt that Anne and the lawyer were formidable forces lined up against him—forces that were intently focused on getting the most favorable terms on their side. After the session, both Anne and Hal were inflamed. For weeks afterward they were edgy, critical of each other, and bickering over the smallest of issues. Their marriage plans were in jeopardy.

Deep Disagreements

Hal now thought that a prenuptial would be degrading to him as a man. Rationally, he could see Anne's point. But emotionally, he felt hurt that she had so little trust in him. He was beginning to think that if she had so little trust now, perhaps they would do better not to get married at all. Above all, he needed to keep his self-respect and some of Anne's demands didn't allow him to do that.

Anne believes that if he *really* loved her, and loved her *just* for her, he would be willing to sign this agreement. After all, it was only a piece of paper. As her lawyers told her, all agreements can be broken. This was just an attempt to set some boundaries that would ultimately be helpful as their relationship progressed. As she saw it, they were going to be together forever, and if he truly loved her and felt the same way, and if his motives were as straightforward as he said, he would sign without hesitation. Anne's trusted advisors were strongly encouraging her not to relent on this. If she began to doubt the wisdom of their position, all she had to do was think of the last rounds with her ex to get her blood boiling and set her resolve.

Partners who demand prenuptial contracts often don't recognize how stressful and emotionally touchy the situation is for their partners. After all, they—the partners with the assets—are in control of the process. They are paying the lawyers and they have the money behind them to feel more confident about their position and security in the world. In the early stages, even the less affluent partners sometimes are not aware of how much emotion they have about the process. Perhaps they are too busy supporting an image of themselves as independent and powerful. They want to hold themselves above the lack of trust their partner seems to be expressing toward them. It might take a few years, but these feelings will eventually surface.

After Anne and Hal tried out their best reasoning with each other and were still not getting anywhere, frustration levels began to increase. As they did, and as the partners tried harder to get each other to "act sensibly" but made no progress, the gloves began to come off. As the next level of this argument emerged, Hal told Anne she was just protecting herself. She had no trust, which was (he observed) one of her problems in life. And he resented being controlled in this way. He resented the fact that her advisors were in the middle of their relationship.

Anne told Hal he was being childish and immature. *He* was being the controller, not her. The reason he didn't have trouble with combining their resources was that he didn't have very much to bring in. It was easy for him to talk! He responded by saying she didn't know how to make money either—she just happened to have an inheritance. She came back to the point that if he really loved her and was not marrying her for her money (as he so loudly proclaimed), he would demonstrate it by signing without delay. And on it went, the argument gradually degenerating in content, each one slamming the other.

Each day the argument headed in the same direction. After restating their positions, both kept repeating them using a lot of different words, as if the other person must somehow be hard of hearing (or a little slow mentally). Each time, before long, they got lost in all the words, wondering how on earth they could have become entangled with a partner who was so defensive and thick. Anne and Hal were now engaged in one of those long, involved, wide-ranging, circular arguments in which nobody listens very carefully. The central issue was supposed to be the prenuptial contract, but all manner of topics (many totally irrelevant) got thrown into the mix. Counterattacks escalated until the point where one or both partners became too frustrated to go any further. A quiet moment or two might follow (as long they avoided the topic), but it kept drawing their attention like a festering sore and before long they were back at it again—off and running down one of those dark alleys. Both said they wanted to get out of the destructive loop they were in, though both seemed unable to sustain any kind of mutually nourishing interaction.

It began to look like the only two options were dodging the issue altogether (and naively hoping it would go away), or signing *anything* to get it over with (which is what many individuals in this position eventually do). We suggested it was too late for the former and quite probably poisonous to allow the latter. The only way *through* now involved some deep soul-searching by both individuals. More feelings were lurking under the surface, feelings that needed to come out into the open before they could have a hope of finding a way through this maze.

What Hal Needs to Know
about Himself

Hal is about to come face to face with two unpleasant aspects of himself. One is his feelings about power and powerlessness; the other is greed.

Powerlessness Hal needs to look at his denial of powerlessness. He has chosen to be with someone who has significantly more money than he has seen in his life, someone who is accustomed to having more of the *kind* of power that comes through having money. He also has chosen someone who has been through the wringer before with a problem marriage and is extra-determined to prevent someone putting a claim on her wealth. Being presented with this agreement is bringing him face-to-face with his powerlessness, and he does not want to see it. He would much rather argue about some fine points of the agreement—or about anything else!

Greed Hal also needs to look at is his greed. A part of him is looking for a shortcut to comfort and power in the world. This is going to be even harder for him to see in himself, as he is wrapped up in the responsible, good-guy persona he has spent years developing. Again, he will argue until he is blue in the face to avoid seeing this aspect of himself! Clearly, there is more in him than greed, but greed is present; and he will need to own it before they can completely move through this problem.

When Doug was facing a similar conflict with Naomi, he said over and over, "I don't want your money. I've gone many years without you and your money and I can easily carry on doing the same. The problem is yours because you are so unwilling to share."

Naomi used to say she wanted full partnership with Doug; she wanted to share her love—and her assets. If it was just her, she would share it all. She needed to protect her money "for her children."

We fought for weeks over this issue and just couldn't get any peace that would last for more than a day or two. Finally, Naomi came out with it. "Admit it! When it comes right down to it, you want all of my money!" Doug had become so frustrated from all the arguing that he blurted out, "You're right. And you don't want to share a penny of it!" Naomi responded, "You're right!" For a minute we stood glaring at each other in silence, absorbing these revealing comments. Finally, we were at one of the core truths underneath our struggles. When we finally heard each other at this very basic level, and it became clear we were willing to accept each other regardless, something important shifted. After that, we had much less need to "prove our points" to each other, as there is no need to fight when you know where you stand. The decision becomes, do you love this person enough to be honest with them? In our situation the clear answer was "yes," and we moved forward.

This kind of direct, non-ego-enhancing communication might seem foreign (and perhaps excessively harsh) to some readers, but we have seen this moment many times with other couples who are giving their all to work through complex issues like these. A great relief is experienced when both partners finally get to their root positions and are liberated from needing to manufacture all manner of fluff to cover them over. From this new position, we had a place of understanding. Finally, we both knew we were hearing something truthful and essential from each other and, unflattering as it was for each of us, we were at a place where we could begin working through this issue in a more honest, real, and constructive way. Love now had a chance to reenter our relationship (an adult love based on reality, not the child's love based on fairy tales, wishful thinking, and denial).

Hal has another problem, which is that he is still in romantic love with Anne (though with the arguments they have been having lately over this agreement, that seems to be changing). Individuals who are in romantic love just do not want to look at this type of material. Yet we can almost guarantee that the moment he truly owns his greed and his desires for easy access to power, the circular arguments are going to stop dead. The question then becomes: Will he and Anne be able to live with this part of the truth?

How do we know that Hal has greed? We know because greed is part of the human drama, and inside, every person has every part of the human drama. Most of us attempt to live our lives according to the highest standards we can and attempt to transcend the baser parts of the human condition, but that doesn't mean we don't all have our shadow sides. To know about our potential for greed and striving to be bigger than that is part of the struggle of life. The person who denies having greed is living behind a mask.

And/And   A person who lives in the simplistic world of either/or will have difficulty not jumping to the conclusion that if Hal is greedy and desirous of power, he must not really love Anne. We hold that the complex and wonderful human drama is much more about "and/and" rather than "either/or." Hal loves Anne *and* he feels greed *and* he is generous *and* he is impatient *and* he is a user *and* he has integrity . . . and so forth. Some of those qualities he is conscious of and some he needs to know more about. Some qualities are easy to accept inside and some aren't. But acknowledge them or not, they exist.

What Anne Needs to Know
about Herself

To move forward in an authentic way here, Anne needs to know who Hal is *and* she needs to know more about herself! Let's take a look at some things Anne needs to become more aware of.

Money Bonds During one of their free-ranging arguments, Hal blurted out that Anne's father was in the middle of their relationship. And he had a point. As long as Anne is tied in with her father, in terms of her inheritance or in any other way, she is bonded to him. A middle-aged woman who is still bonded to her family (or her ex-husband, or anyone else) through money is, without a doubt, acting out more of a daughter role than a mature woman role. This is something Anne needs to look into, because while she is so connected in this way, she has less possibility of bonding with a mate. (If Ann's money had come through her own work, she would still have to look at how she was more bonded to her money than to a potential partner.)

Control and Power Anne also needs to look at her desires for control and power. To be sure, she has met a good match in Hal when it comes to control (they wouldn't be fighting so intensely if that weren't the case); but part of her soul-searching needs to focus on her need for money to sustain an image of power for herself. All partners who demand a prenuptial agreement need to look deep down at their own denied feelings of powerlessness in the world and how much they depend on their assets to prop up their image of themselves. Losing control of assets would bring them face-to-face with this aspect of themselves, and they are highly reluctant to do that.

Greed Anne also needs to look at her selfishness and unwillingness to share what she has—that is, her own greed. Demanding control of the resources that she brings into the relationship might make logical sense; but so long as she is unwilling to share power equally, she won't get what she wants from intimacy and love. No self-respecting partners will forever tolerate a partner who insists on holding the power over them all through a marriage.

One thing Anne might congratulate herself for is having the courage to speak out about her need for a pre-nup soon after the engagement. Some cowards have been known to attempt to slip a pre-nup through just previous to the marriage ceremony.

Finding a Mutually
Acceptable Compromise

With their feelings and thoughts out in the open, Hal and Anne had to find a solution to their dilemma. To their credit, they did.

The stakes were high, and both felt very strongly about their positions. Anne felt she would lose if a prenuptial wasn't signed, and Hal felt like he would lose if he signed anything that would compromise his feelings of personal integrity. At the same time neither partner really wanted the other to lose, because both were aware that starting a lifetime with a mate who felt like the loser in their first major confrontation did not bode well for the relationship. The only way through was a significant compromise on both sides.

In our experience couples who have the courage to bring these types of issues out in the open, find their positions, express feelings, receive feelings, and stay with the situation long enough to become aware of the underlying issues will reach an acceptable compromise—if they truly have an abiding love for one another. The frustrating part is that no one can know what that compromise will be until the issue has been worked through sufficiently. And no one knows how long the process will take. What we do know is that both partners need to be willing to stay in the ring and not collapse or resort to bullying. Both must ultimately be willing to go inward and discover something new—usually not an easy process, because most of the things that are ego-enhancing have already been discovered!

First, both partners must be willing to move off their positions long enough to be able to receive at least some of the partner's experience. Then, especially in a tight conflict such as the one Anne and Hal were facing, both partners have to be willing to give up something of importance to themselves. If all this is done, eventually willingness will develop to negotiate a solution from a more open-hearted position. (And we believe that couples who are *not* ultimately able to get to an open-hearted position over tough issues like these ought be rethinking their commitment.)

Both Hal and Anne had valid concerns, and neither was going to be able to have it totally his or her own way. Hal would be asking too much to demand that Anne unconditionally surrender control of her wealth after knowing him for only a year or so. The reality is that at least one in three marriages doesn't make it past the seven-year mark, and perhaps she would have been foolhardy not to protect herself. She needed time to build trust. We can also see Hal's point about signing away his rights—and his power—to a loved one who is supposed to be entering into the marriage with heart, soul, *and* material well-being.

Hal and Anne eventually decided to seek help from a new lawyer who specialized in mediation. In dealing with volatile issues such as these, hiring a skilled person who is completely neutral to both parties can save a lot of grief. Part of their particular solution was that Hal would sign the prenuptial, but it would contain a sunset clause, meaning if they were together and functioning well after seven years, the contract would terminate. This arrangement gave Anne the safety she needed and Hal didn't feel like he was signing his life away.

Generally, the partner who demands the prenuptial prefers to maintain the ability to choose when (if ever) to terminate the agreement. By doing this, however, he or she sustains an implicit power position and, as we noted before, that will eventually grate on the signing partner. In this case, setting a time limit put both partners on an edge and helped ensure that they would do their best to get clear and make the marriage work for the next few years.

This arrangement took into account the reality that agreements, particularly those around important issues like money, become outdated. They need to be renegotiated from time to time as events change and deeper commitments are called for.

Perhaps Anne was wise to protect her assets at this stage, but if she is still holding onto control in seven years, she is saying she doesn't trust him. It wouldn't bode well for the future of their partnership.

Though the process was difficult, Hal and Anne at least had the courage to duke it out at this stage. On one hand, entering into marriage slightly bloodied and sobered is sad. On the other hand, marriage only gets more challenging. If Anne and Hal hadn't had the patience and stamina to get through this issue, better perhaps that they should have quit in the beginning—and next time look for a partner with equal assets!

Part 4

Relationship
Fitness

12

The Undernourished Majority: The Importance of Talk and Touch

Everything goes easier in a marriage when both partners are getting the attention they want and the nourishment they need from each other. Satisfied individuals give more freely, while depleted ones are inclined to hold back. Happy and fulfilled partners are willing to let the little issues go, and are much less likely to regress into immature responses.

If this is so obvious, why do so many couples neglect each other?

Too many of us today are "running on empty" much of the time. Why do we allow that to happen in our intimate relationships—the one place where we ought to be able to count on getting fueled up? Partners in a second marriage have no excuse for forgetting this rule: *No amount of effort at making any marriage a success can have any lasting effect when partners are regularly in a state of depletion.* If you are serious about keeping each other nourished and happy, read on.

The Need for Talk and Touch

We all know how it begins: He's busy, she's busy, and giving each other attention is one of the first casualties. Unless partners make a conscious effort to do otherwise, they tend to take each other for granted. Many people live in a myth that says a happy marriage "just happens," without anyone having to work very hard at it. Unless their partners are crying out, the assumption is made that they don't need much.

Going to the next level, we discover people have difficulty articulating their needs. Others have a secret belief that their partner should automatically know their needs and be busy filling them without having to be asked. Some have taken in the message they shouldn't have needs at all, or that vocalizing them is not "polite." More than a few just don't take the time to go inward and actually discover what their needs are. In any case, it's a big problem when people either don't know what they need or can't speak up for what they need.

Right now, ask yourself: What are my primary needs in my relationship? What are the two or three things I *really need* from my mate in order to stay healthy and happy in my marriage? What do I need to keep fueled up so I can carry on in life in the most alive way? And if your marriage failed before: What needs of mine didn't get met in prior marriages?

When we ask couples these questions, we usually hear these responses: *love, acceptance, communication, caring, harmony, respect, to be seen, to be heard, to be received, to be needed.* All of these needs are very big. In fact, they are so big they are difficult to measure, so big they take a lifetime to cultivate. In order to keep ourselves nourished as we go along learning about these big needs, what we must have are smaller feeds coming to us on a very regular basis. Going back to the idea that a need not explicitly defined is a need not likely to be regularly met, we have to be able to narrow ourselves down. *What could your partner actually do in your everyday life that would demonstrate to you that your needs are actually being fulfilled?*

Two necessities we hear about almost every time are the *need for talk* and the *need for touch.* With these two needs as the central theme, we thought we would present a micro-analysis of a typical undernourished couple, who have arrived at a point where one partner can't take the starvation anymore. We're picking partners who have already sought help, but are still having trouble making their relationship more nourishing. The surface fixes didn't work for them, and now they are seeking a deeper understanding of what is holding them back from nourishing each other. They could be in their second marriage or their first—their issue is universal enough to cover any marriage.

Sam and Judy: The "Talk Issue"

Sam is the silent type; no extra words from him: Once said is enough. To repeat a thought to a person who is listening to you is an insult to the listener, because you are assuming the person didn't get it the first time. And a message spoken to him more than once is an insult to his intelligence—or perhaps a power play with someone trying to ram a point home. Sam prefers to keep his thoughts inside; he doesn't like to expose them until they are well-formed. For some strange reason, he married a talker.

Judy is getting to middle age and wants more in life. She loves Sam but feels shut out by him. It's as if she is living alone in a marriage. Recently, she has begun to think that if she is alone anyway, she might as well *really* be alone. At least that way she might have a chance of finding a life that sustains her more than the one she is experiencing. A couple of years ago, she and Sam went to therapy, and even though some of the discoveries at that time seemed promising, she is still feeling starved in her marriage. She has reached a point where she feels desperate a lot of the time.

In our session, Judy tells Sam she needs more talk. She wants to know more about his day-to-day happenings, and she needs to know more about what is going on inside him. She also wants him to listen to her more than he does. As things are now, she feels as if she is living with a stone, and she can't take it anymore.

Sam is in a state of alarm. He sees that Judy is really on her way out this time, and he doesn't want to lose her. She's a bit of a yakker, but he loves her dearly. He can appreciate her wanting to get her needs met—he would like to get more of his met, too. But something doesn't seem right to him. This time, instead of keeping his thoughts to himself, over the course of an hour or so in our office, he brings a few of them out in the open.

He feels as if she is asking him to be somebody he isn't. He does a lot of nurturing things for her in his way, things that are often not appreciated. Why can't she accept him for who he is? Why can't she accept what he has to offer instead of trying to change him? She seems to hold him in a position of "never quite good enough." He works hard and talks more than he would like to at work; when he gets home he would just like some quiet. What about *his* needs? Why can't she just get her talk from her woman friends?

Let's stop here for a moment and look in as therapeutic detectives. So far, we have a situation that is not at all unusual in marriage. Two mates who care deeply about each other are caught in an impasse neither one wants to be in. Judy is speaking out an important need—and that's good; she has a right to have her needs met. Sam is making some honest statements about where he stands and that's good; he has a right to have his position heard. In fact, if he would only keep talking like this, we can bet he and Judy will eventually find ways to make their relationship work more effectively. Just by his talking, she would be getting what she is asking for and that level of the problem would be solved; they could then get on with more discoveries and solve more problems. The impasse would eventually get resolved and the marriage would move forward again. But Sam and Judy have been here before, and as soon as the pressure from therapy is off, he goes silent again. When that happens, we can easily predict that everything will, once again, get stuck at the very same point. Since Sam's silence seems to be a major stumbling point in this impasse, we need to know more about what's going on there.

Sam's not stupid—he's heard about Judy's need for more talk for years now. As a practical businessman, he knows that each partner's most essential needs have to be met to keep *any* relationship stable and satisfying. She's not asking him to do something he is incapable of doing (we know this because he talks in the sessions, when the pressure is on him to do so). There must be something going on underneath all this that we don't understand yet because the answer is so obvious: *Find out how much talk she wants and strike a deal.*

If the amount of talk she wants is absolutely too far beyond his capacity and she refuses to negotiate downward, they could end it here and now—and perhaps get on with finding partners who are more compatible. But he has already said he doesn't want to do that. If they could find a way to agree to the amount of talk she is asking for, they could then get on with defining *his* need (just because she spoke up first doesn't mean her needs are any more important than his). If she agreed on that, the logjam would begin to clear and they would be on their way to filling each other up. But none of this is happening either. In fact, this seldom happens in any undernourished relationship.

Let's go inside Sam first. Looking carefully at his statements earlier on, we can see a common thread: Every response is a defense against doing what she wants. Almost every one is a fancy way of saying "No." *He is not conscious of saying "No,"* but it's the message he sends to her, loud and clear. So, take a breath and explore with us a phenomenon most people know about, but don't usually discuss: men's reactivity to women's demands.

Men's Defiance of Women

Okay, men. Try this out. Your partner has just said to you:
"Have supper ready by 6 P.M."
"Clean up your space."
"Take the garbage out."
"Talk to me more."
What is your reaction? What is your feeling?

Many men react defensively when a demand from a woman comes their way. Perhaps this is the product of being born of women or trained by them in the early years; regardless, women somehow get to be seen as "adversaries to be pleased." Pleasing women is all right *on one's own terms,* but acceding to an outright demand is equated with a loss of self, a loss of essential male power, perhaps even a loss of male soul. Men like to play dumb about knowing what women want; but underneath that perplexed expression there is often a hidden intent—a will to preserve self, a will to not "give in" to a woman. It can easily form into a habitual defensive posture, and the name of the feeling that goes along with that posture is *defiance.*

Defiance gives one a sense of power, but it's a phony power. Power based on saying *"No!"* is the power of the toddler just finding his or her way in the world. Because the partner gets defeated (or at least thwarted) as a result of it, postures of defiance might give the *illusion* of personal strength and the preservation of integrity. But the defiant partner is really occupying a position of a fearful young person. (If he weren't fearful of being overwhelmed by her, why would a man like Sam need to reflexively defend against Judy's expression of need?)

As a coping strategy, defiance might work superficially to bolster feelings of "power." In fact, as a way of starting off the development of a self in the earlier years, it's as good a way of coping as any other. The problem occurs when the ingrained defiant strategy carries on past age thirty with little or no updating. A man in his thirties and forties (and beyond) who still reflexively defends against demands from women is kind of sad. Inside his own defensive structure, he believes he is strong, but looking in from the outside you see an underdeveloped man behind a wall. Bolstered maleness behind walls of defense is not a sign of authentic masculinity—it's just a scared person who, deep in his psyche, is simply still back in time, attempting to cope with forces he couldn't deal with head on earlier in life.

If Sam weren't in a position of defense, weren't taking Judy's demand as a threat to his male soul, how might he go about thinking this situation through?

A partner who isn't in defense sees a problem at hand. The mate has a need that has to be met. An adult knows that life is full of demands. An adult is aware that when a man and woman come together for a lifetime, they have to be able to give and take demands from each other on a regular basis (only the child inside would refuse to do this). Sam's mate has a need, one that she has defined as primary to her. Avoiding the issue won't work. Meeting her need is going to require a stretch past a habitual comfort zone into some *dis*comfort. Not meeting one of her most important needs—a refusal to talk more, in his case—will eventually be met by a like response. Two people refusing to provide each other's most important needs become two undernourished people. Two undernourished partners eventually divorce. The outcome is pretty clear. If he wants a successful marriage with Judy, Sam either has to change and stretch past his zone of comfort or change (perhaps in the form of a lost marriage) will eventually be visited upon him. Partners who decide to pull that defiant two-year-old's thumb out of their mouths realize they need to make a study of their mates. Sam might begin to compare his marriage to a business relationship—in order to make it work successfully, you have to know what is important for the other participants. Up to this point, Judy's request for talk has resulted in a knee-jerk reaction and been interpreted by him as nagging. He hasn't opened much to Judy's need because it is not a need he has valued highly himself. Maybe the time has arrived to begin to educate himself more.

The Anatomy of a Talker

Whereas silent types like to take in information through their eyes, talkers have a tendency to take in information through their ears. When faced with a problem, they like to hear the words of the problem, and that obviously requires talking them out. They hear the words that are spoken, take in the information, and process it. As the information is processed, new understandings occur, and that leads to more desire to talk it out. That newer information comes back in through the ears and is processed some more. Looping the data around like this helps talkers arrive at clarity (and ultimately to make sense of the world). Clarity comes faster if words are also received from another person who is exploring the issue. This whole discovery process works better when someone is present to receive the talker's words (who wants to talk to a wall?).

Talking (and listening to talk) is more than a way of learning about the world. It's a sign of caring and respect. It is a way of giving and receiving attention. A type of pleasure can be derived from hashing out an issue (and bypassing the talk in order to jump to solutions cuts some of that pleasure). Regular talk keeps partners up to date with each other and thus better connected. Talk that includes some expression of personal feelings enhances intimacy and truth. Talking helps to keep hearts open, which serves to heighten love.

In short, talk is much more than talk; it is a type of nutrient for a person like Judy. Her demand for more talk does not come from any intent to belittle Sam or steal anything from his soul. It is simply food to her, food she must have to thrive in her relationship.

Silent types like Sam might be inclined to get satisfaction from entirely different endeavors, and that's fine too. It is not as if Judy's way is "right" and his is "wrong." The questions for him are these: Does he want to be with Judy (or anyone like her)? If he does want to be with her, does he want the best she has to offer? Would he rather have it only his way, in his comfort zone, and be in a starved relationship? Or is he willing to give her what she wants and thereby stand a much better chance of getting what *he* wants? As it is, the situation clearly is not working, for he is attempting to live with his single-man habits in a two-person relationship—a marriage. Something has to give.

Defense versus Boundaries

Some of this is starting to get through to Sam, but he's still very cautious. He's hearing Judy more clearly, yet he is still caught in some resistance to her need for more talk. If Sam were to go a little deeper into himself, he would realize that he feels underneath as if Judy has *already* taken over a lot of his life; and if he were to start trying to talk the way she wants him to, there would be no end to it. His fear, deep down, is that she is insatiable. He could be swallowed up by her demands: Give her the talk now and she'll be looking for bigger chunks out of him next month.

If Sam were to carry on in the problem-solving mode begun earlier, he would begin to see that, in order for him to come forward, he would need to have some boundaries defined around her demand. And that would be a big step forward. Up to this point, he has been in automatic defense. The problem is that people who habitually (and thus unconsciously) defend give nothing; they just protect themselves behind a wall. Out of his fear of being devoured by Judy's needs, he hasn't moved in her direction at all. Maybe she would be insatiable, but he can't even find that out for sure until he at least tries to feed her need.

Let's assume that Sam has begun the effort of updating himself and wants to develop more creative and enlivening ways of responding than habitual defense and defiance. He wants to open more to Judy's needs *and* remain true to himself. (We emphasize "and" because, up to now, he has been unconsciously reacting to his situation more in terms of an "either/or" proposition.) Where does he go from here? He must begin learning the fine art of distinguishing between acting defensively and establishing *boundaries*. It's tricky, because these two endeavors often look the same on the outside and, in fact, many people like to fool themselves into believing they are doing one when they are actually doing the other. This is a worthwhile topic to explore, so let's briefly divert our attention in that direction.

Individuals don't need to fear giving up their soul if they know and trust who they are inside and are willing to do the work of establishing clear boundaries. But most of us were not taught about boundaries as children, and we took the easier route of setting up defenses and protective walls around ourselves. Now, as adults, we must learn the difference. True discernment between the two is one of those things that, in real life, is easier to feel than to put in words, but let's give words a try.

Defense and defiance are automatic "No's." When you feel yourself surging up with a reaction to something a partner is bringing to you, the chances are that you are headed toward a defensive response. Setting a boundary, however, is not automatic. Before the boundary is established, pertinent information is received, thoughts *and* feelings are assessed, and real-world considerations are taken into account. Where necessary, you make an effort to describe your boundaries to others. Defense, by contrast, is silent or filled with impersonal words; candid explanations are seldom offered. Boundaries help you and those around you to feel safer, ultimately more relaxed. Defense adds to tension; feelings of mistrust flourish; everyone ends up confused, not quite able to grasp what is happening. Defenses seal the self off, with the net result of making a person less available. Boundaries require a bringing forth of the self, with the net result of making a person more available. Defenses are based on covered-over fear, whereas boundary setting requires courage. People within defenses may "think" they are powerful; people within boundaries don't worry about presenting an image of power; they exude trust in themselves as they are.

A boundary breathes. Though well-defined, it has a degree of permeability. The boundary-setter is not locked into a position, unwilling to renegotiate now and then as circumstances change. A defense is rigid and impermeable. The person behind it is tense, locked in a position, unwilling to take in new information. The face of a person setting a boundary is noticeably different from the face of someone setting up a defensive wall.

If the person who is setting a limit can't discern between defense or boundary, the intimate partner on the other side almost always can. To be on the receiving end of a boundary might be frustrating in the short term, but over the longer term, a relationship becomes more rewarding. The boundary-setter is still available, though in a more defined way. When boundaries are present, partners are freer to be who they really are, feelings of safety and trust build, intimacy deepens, and joy together expands. To be on the receiving end of a defense is just plain frustrating. When one meets defense (or defiance), it feels like a loss of connection. The defender is seldom fully available. When defenses are present, it's hard to know what exactly is going on, trust does not build, and separation ultimately increases.

A defense has many faces but the outcome is always the same. For example, defense might take the form of *stubbornness, fast words, no words, withdrawal, argumentativeness, excuses, counterattacks, good-boy or good-girl behavior, or frozen smiles.* Every one of these reactions tends to be automatic—defenders are just doing what they have always done to protect themselves. The trouble is, the reaction has become so automatic and habitual that the defender has lost sight of other ways of being. In other words, the defensive responding has become so ingrained, defenders usually cannot see how defended they are.

Individuals caught in such a tight system of defense get really stuck; growth in self-awareness is very slow because they have difficulty taking in any information from outside of themselves (everything gets defended off). When these defenses are not challenged, the outcome is always little or no personal growth, and in a marriage, that means stagnation. Intimate partners who can't see past their defensive tendencies end up repeating the same dysfunctional patterns over and over again (without seeing their own role in it).

Boundaries Create Freedom

Finally, Sam is starting to understand the difference between defense and boundaries. He comes to realize that defensive responses go nowhere and, in fact, are destroying his marriage. He comes to realize that, in abandoning his defenses, he need not give up his soul—if he is willing to do the work of establishing boundaries. He realizes that when he engages in negotiations with Judy, he too has a right to speak out his needs. He accepts that some of the time he may need to shift his habitual ways of behaving, but he is beginning to see that possibilities of significant gain are also present.

How does he go about discovering the way to meet her needs without "giving himself away"? This time, instead of nodding in agreement when he really has no intention of following through, or coming up with a lot of words that add up to "No," he tries a new approach. He asks Judy how much talk time she wants.

After she gets over her surprise, Judy says that about twenty minutes a day of honest, direct, eye-to-eye communication would be terrific. Inside himself, Sam is a little shocked that all she wants is twenty minutes. However, rather than agreeing straightaway (and risking saying "Yes" when he doesn't really mean it), he stops and checks inside himself (always a good move when boundaries are being considered). He is willing to give her that talk time, but the truth for him is that right after work, when she seems most to want talk, he would most like some silence. In fact, this has been part of the problem. He feels exhausted coming home and hasn't made the transition out of work yet. When she comes at him for talk, he goes inside his shell to protect himself and, once inside, he finds it difficult to come out again.

He gets clear and speaks. The twenty minutes of talk she describes is agreeable to him, but he'd like half an hour of quiet time after stepping in the door from work—no stress, no pressure to do anything. He describes his need to make a transition into being home. Judy listens and takes in what he has to say. It's interesting information, something she wasn't fully aware of before. It makes sense to her. Okay, she'll give him a quiet space for half an hour after he comes home from work.

Now the ball is in Sam's court. She has offered something to him, and now he needs to come back. He says he'd be willing to talk after supper, and he sets a time to do this. Setting a time is important because that too is a boundary. Partners know what is expected of each other. A lot of people balk at this type of regimentation, but we're looking to change a strong system, built up over many years of ingrained habits of relating. A big effort is required to get new patterns of behavior in motion, and every structure that helps to organize a new behavior is useful at the beginning. Later on, as Sam gets to talking a little more and Judy isn't so starved, they will find a more spontaneous rhythm.

Now boundaries have been established. Both partners know what is required of them. She'll hold off, he'll come forward. They aren't giving their souls away. Twenty minutes of effort doesn't take any superhuman sacrifice. True, he has to give a little bit, but in return he gets some quiet space he can relax into. Judy is delighted at the prospect of getting something from him. She has been so accustomed to his fighting her all the time, hearing him negotiate is like a breath of fresh air. Boundaries are thus creating more freedom for both of them to breathe in their relationship, and the difference in the two of them is noticeable already.

Sam and Judy aren't finished with their negotiation yet, however. In real life, some days or weeks after these types of commitments have been made, they can be out the window faster than New Year's resolutions. When commitments are broken, it's bad news at any stage of a relationship; but when a crisis point is at hand and commitments are broken, the effect is devastating. Partners might not show a reaction to a broken commitment on the outside, but inside their guts, the message sinks in and is felt. "We went through all that and still it broke down." The partner cannot be trusted. The relationship cannot be trusted. When you don't believe your partner will live up to commitments, what's left? Usually only two people who are in it for security. And sooner or later, that's not going to be enough.

With this idea in mind, we always suggest that couples put time limits around their commitments. How long are they absolutely sure they are willing to commit to doing what they say they will do? If necessary, they can make it a shorter time rather than a longer time, since a commitment can always be reimplemented. We suggest this to Sam and Judy, and they agree to try out their talk-related commitment for five days each week, for one month. If the results of the new behaviors are desirable, they can restate or perhaps refine their commitment to something even more desirable. If either of them has been unable or unwilling to follow through for the month, they can stop pretending they are serious about developing a mutually nourishing relationship.

One last reminder: A lot depends on the attitude behind agreements and boundaries. If Sam goes into the talk sessions each time with the spirit of taking bad medicine, he is still essentially in defiance and the potential for gain will diminish in direct proportion.

Sam and Judy Deal with
Needs for Touch

Now that Sam and Judy have hashed through the talk issue and come to some agreement, we go back to Sam. No partner is likely to have the energy to meet a partner's primary need over the long run unless his or her own primary need is being attended to. What is one of Sam's primary needs?

Being the silent type, he is a little slower to articulate his needs, but with a little encouragement he acknowledges that he would like to receive more *touch*. Touch is a primary mode of intimate communication for him, he says, and he needs more of it. The touch doesn't need to be sexual; it can just be stroking, massaging, and rubbing. The most important thing is *regular* touch, some of it without talking.

This time it is Judy's turn to react. She says she tries as hard as she can to do things right. He doesn't appreciate all of the things she does do and all the sacrifices she makes in order to meet his needs. Whatever she does never seems to be good enough in his eyes. She is tired out from all she does. What about *her* need for touch?

Women's Defiance of Men

Now we get a chance to examine the defensiveness of the other side. When a partner comes shooting back like that, what is the net effect of the comments (if we look deeper than just the content of the words)? "No!" No, to your need. Judy is pretty clear about Sam's defensiveness, but has great difficulty seeing her own. Women might appear to have less difficulty fielding demands, but that doesn't make them any less defensive than men. Her "No's" seem just like common sense to her, perfectly justified (just like his seem to him).

The issue of needing touch affects couples differently from the need for talk. In the need for talk, partners tend to polarize against each other, park themselves in opposing camps, and get lost in competing over who is right and who is wrong. One demands and the other defends and both partners get stuck at that spot. In the need for touch, it's not quite the same. Usually both partners are in agreement about the need; they *both* want more touch. Something else gets in their way.

Since we have given defensiveness versus boundaries a good once-over in Sam's material, let's assume that Judy has also learned what she needs to know about that matter. In truth, she was just as caught as Sam, but she now sees the difference between boundaries and defense, and she too is tired of defense. Just as he is becoming aware that his defiance and defensive responses arise from a very young place within him, she is beginning to acknowledge a similar state of affairs regarding herself. Sam has already come forward with a promise of more talk, and now there is no need for her to participate in their long-standing power struggle over who makes the first move. She also says she can fully understand his need for touch and doesn't require any additional information there. However, as she checks inside herself, if she is totally honest, she still finds herself more mouthing the words of being willing to touch than being fully resolved to follow through. What needs to be discovered before she can move past her stuck spot?

Let's go to one of the most challenging parts first. You could ask almost any woman about men's defiance and get recognition of the phenomenon. But ask her where *she* is defiant and you would likely get a blank stare. *She doesn't see it inside herself.* Just as a man is often unconscious of his defiance when confronted by demands from women, women tend to be unconscious of how they defend against men.

Many women, particularly those whose partners are not honoring their primary needs, defy men by refusing to open fully sexually. It's not a conscious act; it's just a way of not losing any sense of power, of preserving a sense of self. It's a refusal to be fully vulnerable. The hidden statement that goes along with it is something like, "I will give you my Mother and I'll sometimes give you my heart, but you won't get my deepest woman. *No!*" It's not that she won't have intercourse, necessarily; it's just that she won't open up to her fullest vulnerability. And when touch becomes routinely associated with sex, touch also becomes a casualty. Again it's not a conscious act of withholding, she just finds herself not touching her partner very much.

Taking this back to Judy and Sam, we can now see this state of starvation between them is a lot deeper than simply two people who are not smart enough to meet each other's primary needs. There's more than a passive process of two individuals simply not knowing any better and having starvation fall upon them. Instead, we see both partners are in defense and defiance, unconsciously playing a role in starving each other out.

We are also beginning to see why the starved situation is so difficult to change in all marriages. When partners are reflexively engaged in defensive postures, they spend no effort at commonsense problem solving. We also begin to see how partners must be willing to know themselves more deeply in order for any real and lasting change to occur.

Another Boundary

Some of these ideas are beginning to ring true to her, but Judy is still cautious. (Alertness to one's own defense structure does not typically arrive in a blinding flash of insight; it takes a lot of time, during which an individual must be willing to make a concentrated effort at self-observation.) She still wants to think it's more Sam's defiance that has led them to this impasse, but she can't ignore what is going on at this moment. He has come forward. She can't just sit back and blame him for this stuck point in their marriage any longer. She is forced to take on some of the responsibility because, right now, further movement depends on *her* coming forward.

The truth is, she would like more touch too, and more intimate sex. But her experience over the past years has been that touch, every time, leads to sex, and that's created a number of problems for her. With her body having learned that touch leads to intercourse each and every time, her body doesn't fully relax into the touch. She enjoys sex, but when touch leads to sex *every* time, she admits she begins to feel "used." She would like to see it this way: more touch, both giving and receiving, sometimes with sex, sometimes just with loving touch for the sake of loving touch. Now the opportunity has arrived for her to create a boundary.

She makes herself clear to Sam: She is willing to make the time to give more touch. She would also like to receive more touch. But she would also like to see some of it be nonsexual— just touch for the sake of touch. As she sees it, touch has been tied to sex through most of their relationship, and her not wanting to go through to intercourse every time has accounted for some of her hesitancy to touch Sam when he asked for it before.

We go back to Sam for his response. Terrific by him. He'd love to have times of just physical touch, like massage, and sometimes touch and sex. The reason this habit has evolved the way it has, as he sees it, is because they weren't having sex very often and they weren't touching very often so the times they did touch usually went to sex.

Judy is a little surprised to hear that he wants some nonsexual touch. She does not quite understand that by making herself too busy to participate in regular touch, she has created a partner who is starved for touch, and that a partner starved for touch tends to react very strongly to it. It's a bit of a revelation to her: Just as she has felt starved, she has also played a role in starving.

Now Judy might say, "Fine, I'll touch you more." If we leave their communication with that as the last word, we can almost guarantee that three, four, or five weeks later, they will be back with about the same level of touch they have today. Why? We must remember that, in general, the forces of everyday life are working against couples' nourishing each other. We get too busy, too distracted, too hungry for power in the world, or too involved with children. Just as with the talking issue, some kind of specific plan needs to be laid out and agreed upon. As our time together ends, we leave Sam and Judy with their negotiation. We sincerely hope they work something out and follow it through, because touch is very important.

The Need for Touch

We cannot overstate the need for regular touch, both sexual and nonsexual, in marriage. Aside from the obvious benefits of relaxation, rejuvenation, and connectedness, touching of all sorts invite partners to come down out of their heads. Once they are in their bodies, their feelings are more accessible. The movement of feelings helps to keep their hearts open, which leads to the heightening of love, which adds to the nourishment of both partners. We all know this is true, and it remains one of life's mysteries why so few follow through with daily touch.

As we have already mentioned, many people (particularly those in first marriages) think that negotiating needs and budgeting time for touch and sex is mechanical and unromantic. In their minds, things should be more natural and spontaneous. Our reply is that partners need boundaries in all parts of their lives if they expect things to happen the way they want them to. If you take an honest look at what actually happens in life when partners refuse to budget time to get needs met, what you usually see is slow starvation mixed in with fantasy ideals that are not being realized.

Allies or Enemies?

In the end, people's needs vary and no one formula can apply to all couples. All couples need to find their own way to a nourishing relationship that includes touch and talk. We can offer cues about how to catch oneself in defense, emphasize the need for boundaries, and provide the basic suggestions for negotiation. But the truth is that all of this won't do a bit of lasting good unless partners make a fundamental determination that applies to and holds all through their relating: they have to decide *whether they are going to come together as enemies or allies.*

In order to act as allies, partners need to start their momentum in a direction that is nourishing for both. Cooperate, apply the energy, and it looks like this: One partner meets the other's needs. A partner who feels nourished is inclined to nourish in return. A relaxed and fed partner is more able to receive. The person who receives gets filled and has more to give. This way of interacting becomes intrinsically rewarding and gains in strength naturally. Lapses in attention pass by without major injury to the relationship because the positive momentum carries both partners through the flat spots.

Somehow (maybe it's too many movies) we don't grasp that this type of positive momentum needs regular input from both partners, sometimes quite a lot if it has been allowed to slow. We also forget that it can turn just as easily in the opposite direction: One partner doesn't meet the other's primary needs, and that second partner eventually responds in kind. Partners begin power struggles over who should make the first move and meet the other's needs first. As they struggle, both partners get hungrier. Nobody wants to go inside and feel. Rather than coming out, the partners withdraw. In a starved and stressed condition, they revert to childish stances and defenses against demands. It sounds pretty pathetic, but if you have been through a failed marriage you know how easily it can happen.

The question is, how does a couple get the momentum going in the direction of mutual benefit? Talk and touch routines can be the beginning of supplying mutual food to grow the relationship. When partners feel nurtured, they become allies and begin a real partnership. It's as simple as caring for a plant: Water it, feed it, and it grows. Starve it and it dies. Intimate relationship is no different.

13

The Dance
of Intimacy:
It Takes Two
Individuals

A second marriage that is alive and vibrant requires two people who are not only *partners,* but *individuals* in their own right. For most of this book we've discussed what we call the "couple's issues"—issues for which *both* partners have joint responsibility: agreements, relating skills, feelings exchange, power and control issues, reciprocity of needs, and learning how to get the most out of gender differences. Not surprisingly, these are also the issues that get the most attention in couple's literature. But they are only half the story. Successfully dancing the dance of intimacy takes two well-developed *individuals.*

Know Yourself

"Individuals' issues" have to do with what individual partners must undertake in order to contribute to a successful marriage. For example, the partners have unique personal histories that they bring with them into a relationship, and each must work out his or her own unresolved material. Each individual has to take personal responsibility for consistently showing up in the marriage with a *well-defined self*. Further, each individual is responsible for *maintaining* that self within the relationship.

We're not talking about a self that is sustained through defense or bolstered egocentricity. Everybody has one of those. We are not talking about the "me-generation" type of self derived from number-one-first attitudes or obsessive self-centeredness. Those selves are not so difficult to build, either.

Individuals with a well-defined self know what they are feeling from moment to moment. People who are "inside themselves" in this way trust themselves enough to express their thoughts and feelings to their intimates. They don't need to adopt the feelings of their partner to feel alive, nor do they need to shut off another's thoughts and feelings in order to feel safe. They organize time for introspection and inner study because they know that inner awareness does not evolve without continued effort. They realize that self-awareness is an ongoing process and to think they already know everything about themselves is the most dangerous form of ignorance.

People who know themselves at the deeper levels have no need for automated defenses when in the presence of their intimates. They have no need to defy their partner in order to preserve a sense of personal identity or integrity. Partners who have a strong sense of self (again, we don't mean a *defended* self) take full responsibility for whatever is going on in their marriage.

In the case example that follows, we will follow a typical couple who did not keep up with their inner development as individuals and found themselves, years later, overly merged in a lifeless marriage. Working on couple's issues alone was not enough for them because as individuals they didn't have—and *were not aware of not having*—well-defined selves. We hope their circumstance will inspire you to keep up with doing the work of self-building.

Dennis and Caroline:
Poorly Defined Selves

Dennis and Caroline were married for twenty-three years. During this time they did all they needed to do to raise a family, and they shared many caring and rewarding experiences. Now their children were out in the world, and Dennis and Caroline had more free time then ever—along with the financial stability to enjoy it. They had found a measure of success in their community and, from all of the surface evidence, ought to have been experiencing the time of their lives. But, in fact, their marriage was flat and unfulfilling. Both had the sense there must be more to life, but neither talked much about it.

Then Dennis and Caroline attended their friends' wonderful twenty-fifth wedding anniversary party, and came face to face with the poverty of their own relationship. They realized that *they* could not get up in front of family and friends and honestly say such sweet words or look so lovingly at each other had it been *their* twenty-fifth. Their disappointment and sadness crystallized into a determination to bring some life back to their relationship. They knew it wasn't going to be easy. They set a date, a year away, and made a commitment to give it their all until that date. If, by then, they couldn't restore their marriage to the point where they could authentically celebrate togetherness on their twenty-fifth, they would proceed with divorce. The couple who seemingly had it all would be ready to admit they had very little, if anything, left. This new commitment itself was enough to get some spark going, but how were they to proceed from here?

Finding the Truth

Dennis and Caroline must find the truth of what their relationship *is* in order to embark on an authentic journey to where they would like to be. This is one of the most difficult and time-consuming tasks they'll face, because the truth in a situation like this is bound to be painful. A twenty-three-year relationship that has led to such a lifeless state of affairs is a disappointing experience. Both partners contributed to the decline, and both will need to examine parts of themselves that aren't particularly enhancing to their self-image.

The first thing Caroline said was that she couldn't stand Dennis's *neediness*. She had been a mother for her children all those years, and she felt overwhelmed by his neediness, which had been growing as he got older. She could barely take care of her own needs, let alone his. Dennis was so self-centered. And what about *her* needs? She just found herself closed off to him.

Dennis felt that Caroline was so critical and difficult to please that he just gave up. The greatest part of her affection had gone to the children. In earlier years he tried, in a lot of ways, to spark things up between them. But whenever he came forward, she found fault with him. Whenever he stood up for something he believed in, she would judge him. He knew that saying so sounded kind of silly, but Caroline almost seemed not to want him to *have* an identity separate from her—and yet she regarded him derisively for merging with her.

As therapists, our choice was either to go back and forth between Dennis and Caroline for about forty rounds of recriminations and slowly help them to find their way to what was going on . . . or go directly to some of the root issues. Since recriminations like these are only exciting for the participants themselves, let's skip over that part and go straight to the roots and see what we could learn.

Looking on as objective observers, we see two emotionally numb partners who have not been nourished well by their relationship for years. We can confidently predict that all kinds of feelings are stuffed below the surface. We see each person talking almost exclusively about the other and we can bet it is a long-standing habit. When partners talk about the other in this fashion, we know blaming and defensiveness is the usual order of the day. In general, we see a marriage between two souls *who haven't been able to hold onto themselves as individuals, separate from each other.* Thus, they have become lost *in* each other, merged into an undifferentiated, passionless mush.

Let's examine these ideas one at a time.

Blaming and Defensiveness

Blaming is a killer in marriage. The worst part is that it becomes habitual—partners are unconscious of how blaming and defended they have become. As Dennis and Caroline attempted to unravel their knotted marriage, almost every second statement started with something like "You are . . ." or "You do . . ." or "You did . . ." or "You didn't do . . ." or "If only you . . ." or "I can't believe you . . ." or "I tried . . . but you . . ."

and so forth. Virtually the entire effort of the participants in that kind of exchange is directed at placing the focus on the other. And in the heat of interaction, neither of the partners makes much of an attempt to practice coming consistently from within themselves (in fact, they are not even conscious of how out of themselves they really are). Another way of saying it: They don't really know what they are doing.

If we get right down to it, partners who habitually blame have become entrenched in victim positions. The victim in an intimate relationship is like a child who believes all unpleasant events and feelings are due to outside causes: "It's not my fault." When the victim part of us is running our show, practically all of the effort we make gets directed toward pinning blame on our partner. The victim habit contributes greatly to the decline of the marriage in the first place, and when a relationship enters a wobble, the victim can really take off.

These internal victims have been operating below the surface for many years, each secretly viewing the other as the main cause of dysfunction in the marriage. Since neither Dennis nor Caroline has been paying enough attention to their internal beings, they have unthinkingly supported the benevolent fiction that their marriage was just "fine." As they begin to penetrate the fiction, one of the first hidden aspects to come out in full force is this victim, who wants to point the finger at the other for all the major problems. If they don't each resolve to take more personal responsibility for keeping self-aware, they could easily get stuck at this stage (as many couples do).

Dennis and Caroline have no real hope of getting anywhere together while they are entrenched in this blaming/victim defense structure. The blaming habit is resistant to change and is quite likely to take a long time to shift totally, though some start must be made with it early on. It is one of the roots they must begin to examine seriously.

When Dennis and Caroline were first presented with the idea that they both had firmly entrenched themselves in victim positions, they were shocked. Neither had been aware of acting from a victim mentality. They had never even considered the possibility before. But when their attention was brought to it, they both had a hard time denying the number of times they were caught in "you statements" in regard to each other. As they became more aware of the number of "you statements" each made, they gradually became more conscious of how little they were in touch with themselves. Just cultivating this awareness is a big part of the shift that needs to happen.

Dennis and Caroline made a good first step with their commitment to explore their relationship for a year. But as we often point out, adopting the victim role is *a very big habit,* and for them to stop doing it on their own would have proved extremely difficult. When partners are not self-aware, they tend to be hyper-reactive to each other. Instead of recognizing that they each need to cut the blaming for their own good, *regardless of what the other says or does,* they get caught in reacting to the other. One points the finger; the other, not having a self, almost instinctively reacts and points the finger back. The other reacts to that and off they go, competing in blame, competing in defensiveness.

Individuals who are truly aware of themselves and their feelings recognize that their blaming needs to stop, period. To adopt the victim stance in any of life's endeavors is ultimately damaging to self. If the other partner carries on with blaming, that is that individual's problem. Countering in like fashion is hurtful to oneself. In a marriage between individuals who are growing, when one stops the blaming, the other will eventually drop his or her defense as well. Then partners get a chance to discover more about who they really are—the marriage goes forward. If one partner begins refusing to blame and the other continues to blame without interruption, the outcome becomes clear. Their marriage is over. Learning to hold back from blaming in favor of checking inside for whatever one is feeling at the moment is a lot easier to talk about than to carry out, but it must happen if a stagnant marriage is be fully revived.

Once again, pulling back the pointing finger of blame and learning how to express from the inside is much easier when some mutually respected, neutral person is there to catch the blaming every time it happens (which at the beginning is a lot!). Dennis and Caroline could have asked a friend to monitor them for hours at a time and to intervene when appropriate, but friends like that are hard to find. They needed a trained specialist to help them through this stage.

If you are resistant to the idea of seeking and paying for help, we invite you to take the challenge now—*before* a crisis develops. Watch yourself for the beginnings of blame. Whenever you find yourself talking about your partner, or worst of all, telling him or her who he or she is, catch yourself. Chances are you may be subtly attempting to shift responsibility over to your partner, and that is the beginning of blame. Take note of the number of times you use the world "you" in your sentences, particularly when some kind of contentious issue is arising. In a stuck marriage, "you" statements are deadly (unless they are, perhaps, "You are wonderful, good-looking, and sensitive.").

When Dennis and Caroline started to work with blame, they began to learn about how much they use blaming as a way of defending themselves. They resolved to pay more attention— which was another good step. But where could they go from there? They had to begin opening up their emotions.

Emotional Numbness

Making a determined effort not to blame is not sufficient in it-self. (In fact, a sophisticated person could turn that into an-other form of defense: "I'm not the blamer here. But I do silently judge *you* for being one.") Partners must train them-selves in ways to bring their inner selves forward (an individ-ual's issue) and learn about feelings exchange (a couple's issue).

Clearly, couples in Dennis and Caroline's position have lost their passion. They get along from day to day, but they have also become rigid. As we noted earlier, a major cause for loss of passion is stuffing difficult feelings. It is certainly not difficult to imagine that after twenty-three years, particularly now that their marriage is teetering, Dennis and Caroline have big feel-ings of anger and resentment.

Expressing resentments and learning to bring out long-buried anger in constructive ways is also not done overnight. But feelings must be opened up before the partners can dis-cover whether enough passion is present to bring a relationship back to life. Since Dennis and Caroline made a commitment to give themselves one year, they had no excuse to avoid some feeling skills training, much like we described in the earlier chapters in this book. Having come to realize that feeling skills would help them whether they stayed together or not, they committed to developing that area during their trial year.

For them, it started slowly. They began by bringing out re-sentments. This is tough at the beginning; but for a couple who still care for each other, getting resentments into the open in a contained, direct way, in front of witnesses, eventually leads to relief and softening. (If it doesn't, it's a good sign the end is coming.) When long-standing resentments, both big and little, are expressed and received, couples are able to get on with discovering more emotions in their marriage. (Severely stuck couples have great difficulty listening for more than a few seconds without preparing a defense. Once again, for those partners, we highly recommend professional help for this type of clearing.)

We start off with resentments because partners are usually willing to talk about past resentments and grievances. But the feeling behind resentments is really anger. Passionless partners who have a desire to become unfrozen with each other must learn how to express and receive anger. Anger is not the end-all and be-all of feelings training, but it is the first place most people get stuck. Refusing to deal with anger eventually results in a diminishment of the rest of the feelings. When partners open up to their anger, the rest of the feelings, the rest of the passion, comes much more easily.

Working with their long-stuffed anger was another big challenge for Dennis and Caroline. Anger is a difficult feeling for most couples, but it is particularly challenging for individuals who don't have a real self. When you don't have a self, anger can be terrifying. Dennis and Caroline were so afraid of anger that they had pushed it away and denied it. People who don't deal with their anger either find themselves blowing it out with attacking words, acting it out in passive ways, or going numb. Dennis and Caroline agreed that they did all these things. Since they had committed to doing all they could, they decided to acquire some anger skills. They discovered that once they learned the basics of expressing and receiving anger, they had little to fear from feelings, and the other feelings came much more easily. When the other feelings came, they opened up more, got more into truth, had a little more excitement, and eventually got a clearer insight into whether they wanted their marriage or not.

If you don't want this kind of deadness in your marriage, pay attention to resentments as they are in the process of building. If you find that you are mumbling to yourself about some grievance, be alert. If you find yourself avoiding some topic or closing off in some way, check inside. If you find yourself swallowing anger or rationalizing it away, be extra alert. If you do not become aware of these patterns, you are setting the stage for a crisis in your marriage.

Two Lost Selves in a Marriage

The story of Dennis and Caroline was familiar. At the very beginning of their relationship, neither really knew who they were at the deepest levels. Early on, Caroline became immersed in the children and developed an identity as a mother. Dennis developed a self on the basis of who he was in his career. As they both became highly involved in doing for others and keeping very busy, they learned to *play the role* of having a self. Occupied as they were by things outside themselves, neither spent much effort discovering what was going on inside. Side by side as parents and spouses, they did what needed to be done, some of which produced wonderful results. But neither shared much of their inner world with the other, in large part because they hadn't developed an inner awareness enough to be able to articulate it.

When the children left home, and their careers became less demanding, Dennis and Caroline were left with each other but not a lot to share that was challenging or meaningful. If they had been developing their inner selves during all their years together and had practiced at sharing with each other from that level they would now be in the ideal position to enjoy many interesting and growing years with each other. Instead they found themselves bound up in knots, full of blame, and much more prepared to defend than grow. As we have said in many ways, this is a typical outcome for people who don't do feeling work because: when you don't know how you feel it is impossible to know who you really are.

Married partners who haven't developed inner selves tend to be highly reactive to each other. Rather than consistently expressing personal inner truth, each is hyper-reactive to what the other says. When two are playing this game, he reacts to her reacting to him reacting to her. She reacts to him reacting to her and so on. Both partners are very absorbed in this drama, but so much confusion obstructs the most important message: Nobody is home! It is a somewhat frightening scenario and children of parents who are playing this game pay a real toll.

This is a difficult situation to address because *neither partner is aware they don't have a grounded self to offer the other.* When neither partner is "home," and both are simply reacting to the other, all they can see is what the other is doing *to* them. Not having a real self, and not having practice at generating true feeling consistently from the inside, life seems to be coming at them from the outside. From their blinded position, they conclude that the cause of *who* they are and of *what is happening to them* in their marriages must also be coming from the outside. Taking that a step further, the conclusion is obvious: each is certain that the other must be responsible for any difficulties they are having. That's about as far as they can go until a major shift happens within each of them as individuals.

Finding Themselves

How did Dennis and Caroline tackle this problem? First they acknowledged that their deeper selves were not as well developed and defined as they could be. This discovery, too, did not occur overnight. Until they brought to awareness the amount of blaming and defensiveness they engaged in, and until they became more aware of how lacking they were in feeling skills, neither had any idea they didn't have a developed self. They just seemed to be deadlocked in some kind of hopeless marriage, with no way out.

In the beginning of their exploration, even entertaining the idea they could have reached this point of presumed maturity without a fully developed self was almost laughable. Now, after a little more effort at discovery, the recognition that *they had lived more than half their lives this way* was deadly serious. They began to recognize if they, as individuals, *had* a self—a self who knew what it felt from moment to moment, a self who knew what it needed, a self who could express honestly, a self who was able to receive the other—*they wouldn't be in this dead relationship.* That was a stunning awareness, one that produced their first believable hint that something other than struggle and divorce was possible for them in the future.

Dennis and Caroline reached a point in their discovery that all couples going through this type of reevaluation experience. They could opt for some smaller fixes and perhaps patch up their marriage for another few years. Or they could decide on a major overhaul. The only long-term answer we know for partners who have lost themselves in a marriage is to dedicate considerable effort—months and years—to finding their deeper selves. We call this "building a container." We believe it is the work *all* partners in intimacy must, in one form or another, eventually take on in order to sustain rich intimate lives.

Having declared themselves to be serious about getting their marriage back on track, Dennis and Caroline decided to take it on. How did they undertake this part of the journey?

Building a Container

All fulfilling relationships require two fully present human beings, each of whom is "inside his or her own container." What do we mean by "container"? It is where you and you alone live. It is inside your body. It has boundaries. It is like a bottle or basket inside your body. It is the place within our bodies where we can hold our feelings, desires, intentions, and everything else that makes us who we are.

One of the ways you can begin your discovery is to make the effort regularly to hold in check your impulse to keep on "doing," find a quiet spot, sit down, and begin to pay more attention to your inner edges. Try it now. Close your eyes and pull all of your energy inside. If you find that your center of awareness is up near your eyes and won't budge from that location, try letting your "eyes" sink down, down through your throat, and locate them somewhere around your heart. To the rational mind this might sound like a silly thing to do, but you can't know anything for sure unless you try it out a few times. When you are able to bring your eyes down like this and hold this state of being for a few minutes, notice the difference— "looking" from here versus looking out from your eyes. We call this looking from your "inner" eyes.

When you feel more at ease doing this little exercise with your eyes closed, open your eyes and look out. The first few times, most people find that their center of awareness jumps straight back into their heads, and they begin almost immediately to judge, analyze, and react to outside stimuli. But if you keep up your practice, you will begin to be able to feel a difference as you look more from those "inner" eyes.

Here's another simple exercise. As you look at and engage your partner, try holding a piece of your attention on the bridge of your nose at the same time you are looking. This is not too difficult to do when you make up your mind to do it, but try keeping it up for more than a minute or two. Try and do it when you are dealing with some contentious issue between the two of you! You will discover that the habitual way—the way you have practiced most of your life—is to be outside of yourself, focused entirely on the other person, not having yourself in the picture at all. In looking from what we might call "regular" sight, one's mind is automatically oriented toward interpreting and reacting to events outside of oneself. As you learn to look from inside your own container, with an awareness of what is going on inside you, you begin to perceive things in an entirely different way, a way you likely didn't even know existed before.

Container-building work is much easier to talk about than to do; but, like anything else, it goes a lot faster if you bring attention to it on a daily basis. The next time you are with your intimate, try pulling all of your energies in before you begin a conversation. When some strong issue comes up, practice holding a piece of your intention on your own physical boundaries. Try closing the physical distance and then opening it. Periodically ask yourself what are you feeling? Notice how quickly you forget to do any of this, which is a reflection of how easily you slip outside of yourself. Here's the rule of thumb: *If you are not aware of being inside yourself, you probably aren't.*

Doing this type of work takes a lot of effort—more than you might imagine at the beginning. However, as you practice this more, a new habit slowly develops. Ever so gradually it becomes intrinsically self-reinforcing, and the renewed excitement in intimacy makes it all worthwhile.

Six Important Tasks

In our study of container-building during the past dozen years, We have recognized six major components or tasks:

1. *Set aside time each day to locate and be with your inner self.* In order to locate and build on your inner self, you must

pay regular attention to it. We are not talking about retreating to the contemplative life on a remote mountain-
top—you must make the effort to build regular time for
introspection into your life. Twenty minutes set aside
every day, sitting or walking, practicing with "eyes inside," can lay the foundation for a new way of being with
yourself and your intimates.

2. *Become involved in an ongoing creative endeavor that is not
for profit or power.* Creativity connects you to your inner
life in a very direct way. Want to know more about your
feelings? Try drawing them. Stretch yourself by attempting a creative mode you are not practiced at. For example, if you are a writer, try sketching or painting. If you
know a lot about music, try sculpting. One of the keys is
keeping up with the creative process on a regular basis,
say at least once a week.

3. *Complete things that are unfinished.* Most people's contain-
ers are stuffed with unfinished business from the past, including old bonds and unexpressed feelings. The work
begins with your willingness to bring out these old,
blocked experiences to help you open up the self. After
years of experience with this kind of work, we have seen
that it almost invariably ends up focusing on healing with
families of origin.

4. *Set an intention to become more alert to your own defenses.*
Your defenses are the protective walls you have built up
over the years. They probably served you well in the first
half of your life, but in the second half, when they are habitually deployed in your intimate relationship, they lead
to a deadening of feelings and aliveness. The goal is not to
live without defenses, but to learn how to choose appropriately *when* to use them. Defenses are only a problem in
intimacy when partners are so habitual in their defended-
ness that they don't know of any other way of being.

5. *Focus on developing increased feeling awareness.* Especially,
learn how to locate, express, and receive feelings. Review
the chapters on feelings training if necessary.

6. *Take care of your body.* Building a container in a neglected physical body is difficult. Younger minds believe they will be around forever, riding around on top of bodies that are virtually maintenance-free. Older bodies, if we listen to them, regularly remind us of the need for attention to diet and a regular fitness regime.

In this chapter we have chosen as a case example a couple who are in a crisis. Why didn't we select a nice, sweet success story? Because creating highs is relatively easy, but those kinds of highs don't last. The real work of intimacy requires deliberate, sober, day-to-day attention and work. Everyone has been around couples like Dennis and Caroline—and do you know what? Slipping into a blaming, overly merged, emotionally flat relationship happens very easily. Deep down, these partners probably knew early in their marriage that they should be spending more effort at strengthening their relationship, but things just slipped away from them. They can still work it out now—we've seen many who returned to more passion than they would have imagined possible—but what if they had started earlier? What if most or all of their twenty-three years together had been spent in passion, discovery, excitement, and aliveness instead of sleepy inattention to their inner beings? In the end, the issue may not so much be whether an apparently failed relationship can be resurrected, for many can, but whether those many years, now lost and wasted, might have been better spent in taking on life in its fullness.

We challenge you to start now. And start with what you can *do* now, this very moment: Begin to find your self so you have more to contribute to your marriage. If our container-building image doesn't work for you, find some other way of taking on the process of developing your inner self. Update your commitments to each other. Make a date to clear out resentments when you sense heaviness setting in. Try out some kind of couples' training at least once a year (and allow yourself to be a student in this most challenging of life's endeavors). Don't let yourself fall into lazy assumptions about "happily ever after," since, as you ought to know by now, it doesn't happen that way.

The Final Word:
Priorities

None of the material in this book will stand a chance of making your second marriage a success if you, as a couple, don't take a hard look at your priorities. In marriages that break down, partners invariably choose work, children, friends, and family over their spouse. Somewhere deep in their unconscious, these partners believe their marriage will hold no matter what. That's not only sloppy thinking, *it's not true*. This belief goes back to the expectation that mommy and daddy will be there, no matter how you behave or how little you give of yourself to another. But husbands and wives are intimate partners, not parents. If both partners won't agree to put their relationship first, nothing can keep the marriage passionate, nourishing, and ultimately intact.

Sometimes you, as intimate partners, must put your commitments to each other aside. But if you do this more often than you nourish each other with talk, touch, attention, and feelings, you might as well give up on a fulfilling relationship right now. If you *are* willing to commit to each other and reprioritize, your second marriage can be all you want it to be. It's up to you now, and we wish you all the best!

Index

About the Authors

Doug and Naomi Moseley currently conduct workshops for couples and individuals at their retreat centers in Taos, New Mexico, and British Columbia, Canada. In addition they present lectures and seminars and offer weekend workshops in other parts of the United States and Canada. For information about their current schedule, contact them at:

P.O. Box 540
Arroyo Hondo, NM 87513
(505) 776-1074

www.moseley@plaza.org